Die hauptsächlichen Gedanken der Relativitätstheorie.

Fragt einen klugen, aber nicht gelehrten Mann, was Raum und Zeit seien, so wird er vielleicht so antworten. Wenn wir alle körperlichen Dinge, alle Sterne, alles Erdreich aus der Welt fortgenommen denken, dann bleibt so etwas wie ein ungeheures Gefäss ohne Wände übrig, das eben als „Raum" bezeichnet wird. Es spielt gegenüber dem Weltgeschehen dieselbe Rolle wie die Szene zur Theatervorstellung. In diesem Raume, diesem wandlosen Gefäss gibt es ein ewig gleichmässig ablaufendes Tik Tak, das allerdings nur Geister, diese aber überall vernehmen können, das ist die Zeit. Diese Auffassung vom Wesen von Raum und Zeit hatten die Naturforscher in der Hauptsache bis auf unsere Tage, wenn sie derselben auch keinen so kindlichen Ausdruck gaben, als wir es soeben der Einfachheit wegen gethan haben.

Auf Grund dieser Auffassung ist man geneigt, Aussagen von folgender Art einen unmittelbaren Sinn zuzugestehen. Zwei Ausbrüche des Vesuv fanden zu verschiedener Zeit, aber an demselben Orte statt (nämlich am Krater des Vesuv). Das Aufleuchten zweier entfernter, „neuer Sterne" findet zu derselben Zeit aber an verschiedenen Orten statt. Seit Langem weiss man, dass die Aussagen der ersten Art (über die Gleichörtlichkeit) keinen Sinn haben. In der That dreht sich ja die Erde um ihre Achse, bewegt sich dabei um die Sonne, und bewegt sich mit dieser noch obendrein nach dem Sternbilde des Herkules hin. Man kann also doch nicht ernsthaft behaupten, dass beide Ausbrüche des Vesuv an demselben Orte des Weltalls stattgefunden hätten. Man sieht an diesem Beispiele leicht, dass wir derartigen Aussagen über Gleichörtlichkeit überhaupt keinen Sinn beimessen können. Wir können nur sagen: die beiden Ausbrüche des Vesuv fanden an demselben

Orte in bezug auf die Erde statt. Die Erde spielt in dieser Aussage die Rolle eines „Bezugskörpers". örtliche Aussagen haben nur dann einen Sinn, wenn sie auf einen Bezugskörper bezogen werden.

Im Gegensatze scheinen aber Aussagen über Gleichzeitigkeit überhaupt über Zeiten einen Sinn zu haben, unabhängig von jedem Bezugskörper. Man ist zunächst geneigt, einen Menschen für geisteskrank zu erklären, der behauptet, die Aussage vom gleichzeitigen Aufleuchten zweier Sterne hätte keinen bestimmten Sinn, wenn man nicht einen Bezugskörper aufweise, auf den sich die Aussage über Gleichzeitigkeit beziehen solle. Und doch ist die Wissenschaft durch die überzeugende Gewalt von Erfahrungsthatsachen dazu gezwungen worden, dies zu behaupten. Wie kommt dies?

In diesem seltsamen Ergebnis führten die Erfahrungen über die Ausbreitung des Lichtes. Auf Grund vieler Experimente kamen die Physiker zu der Überzeugung, dass sich das Licht im leeren Raume mit der Geschwindigkeit $c = 300\,000$ km pro Sekunde fortpflanze, und zwar ganz unabhängig davon, mit welcher Geschwindigkeit der Körper bewegt ist, welcher das Licht aussendet. Man denke sich etwa einen Lichtstrahl, den die Sonne in einer bestimmten Richtung aussendet. Derselbe legt nach dem eben ausgesprochenen Gesetz pro Sekunde den Weg c zurück. Man denke sich nun, dass die Sonne dem Lichtstrahl einen Körper nachschleudere, der sich in derselben Richtung mit der Geschwindigkeit 1000 km durch den Weltraum bewegt. Das ist leicht zu denken. Nun können wir uns den abgeschleuderten Körper ebenzeigt als Bezugskörper gewählt denken und fragen uns: mit was für einer Geschwindigkeit pflanzt

sich der Lichtstrahl fort für das Urteil eines Beobachters,
der nicht auf der Sonne, sondern auf dem abgeschleuderten
Körper sitzt? Die Antwort scheint einfach: Wenn
ausgeschleuderte Körper dem Licht mit 299000 km Geschwindigkeit nacheilt, so hat indessen die Lichtstrahl gegen
diesen um 299000 km in der Sekunde vorwärts, schwer
wäre es, wenn der Lichtstrahl nicht von der Sonne sondern von dem ausgeschleuderten Körper ausgesandt
würde; denn wir wissen ja dass die Lichtgeschwindigkeit nicht vom Bewegungszustand der Lichtquelle
abhängig ist.

Dies Ergebnis macht misstrauisch. Sollte sich das
Licht vom abgeschleuderten Körper aus tatsächlich
wirklich anders ausbreiten als von der Sonne
aus. Sollten die Gesetze der Lichtausbreitung
abhängen vom Bewegungszustande des Bezugskörpers? Dann würde es in der Welt etwas wie absolute Ruhe
geben. denn man könnte so argumentieren. Indem auf
beliebig bewegte Bezugskörper (hier der ausgeschleuderte
Körper) pflanzt sich das Licht mit verschiedener,
und zwar von der Richtung abhängiger Geschwindigkeit fort. Dann gäbe es Bezugskörper von ganz bestimmten Bewegungszustande, inbezug auf welche vielleicht
das Licht mit der nach allen Richtungen gleichen
Geschwindigkeit c fortpflanzt. Solche Bezugskörper
würden aus mit gutem Rechte als absolut ruhend bezeichnen können (in unserem Überlegungsfalle die Sonne). Gibt
es wirklich solche absolute Ruhe in physikalischen Sinne?
Hängen die Naturgesetze wirklich vom Bewegungszustande
des Beobachters bezw. des Bezugssystems ab, wie es die
obige Überlegung über die Lichtausbreitung zu fordern
scheint?

Die Erfahrung spricht dagegen. Wenn wir uns in einem gleichmässig fahrenden Eisenbahnwagen befinden, merken wir

nicht der Fahrer des Wagens. Alle physikalischen Experimente
gelingen in einem solchen Wagen (oder in einem gegen die
Erde ruhenden Hause. Die physikalischen Experimente,
die man auf der Erde anstellen, zeigen keine Wirkungen der
Bewegung an, welche die Erde mit allen auf ihr befindlichen
Gegenständen ausführt. Allgemein: Die Naturgesetze sind
unabhängig vom Bewegungszustande des bezugskörpers.

Diese Aussage bezeichnet man kurz als Relativitätsprinzip.
Aber wir können doch aus unserer obigen Überlegung folgern zu
müssen gelangt, dass bezüglich der Gesetze der Lichtfort-
pflanzung dies Relativitätsprinzip nicht gelte; wie steht
es damit in Wahrheit? Der Amerikaner Michelson bewies
vor weit als 30 Jahren durch sein berühmtes optisches Experiment dass das Relativitätsprinzip auch für die Lichtausbreitung gelte; in einem Falle, in dem die Theorie
einen Einfluss der Erdbewegung auf den Verlauf des Ex-
perimentes voraussehen liess.

Die Überlegung musste also einen Fehler enthalten.
Das Gesetz der Lichtausbreitung ist genau das gleiche, ob man
der Sonne oder den abgeschleuderten Körper als bezugskörper
wählt. Der Lichtstrahl legt sowohl gegenüber der
Sonne als auch gegenüber dem von ihr mit 1000 km
weggeschleuderten Körper 300 000 km per Sekunde
zurück. Wenn dies unmöglich scheint, so beruht dies nur
auf der falschen Hypothese von dem absoluten Charakter
der Zeit. Eine Sekunde von der Sonne aus beurteilt ist
nicht eine Sekunde von dem ausgeschleuderten Körper aus
beurteilt.

Es gibt in der Welt kein überall hörbares Tik-Tak, was
man als Zeit bezeichnen könnte. Wenn die Physik von der Zeit
reden will, so muss sie dieselbe erst definieren
durch eine Vorschrift, wozu man für diese Definition
notwendig eines Bezugskörpers bedarf, und dass die Definition
nur in Bezug auf einen gewählten bezugskörper Sinn hat. Es zeigt

weil, dass man inbezug auf einen Bezugskörper die Zeit so definieren kann, dass inbezug auf ihn und die definierte Zeit das Gesetz von der Lichtgeschwindigkeit gültig ist. Diese Definition lässt sich für beliebig bewegte Bezugskörper beliebigen Geschwindigkeitszustandes durchführen. Aber es zeigt sich, dass die Zeiten verschiedener bewegter Bezugskörper nicht miteinander übereinstimmen. Man findet dies genauer begründet in meinem gemeinverständlichen Buche über Relativitätstheorie an verschiedenen Orten stattfindend, (   ). Sind zwei Ereignisse von einem Bezugskörper aus beurteilt gleichzeitig, so sind sie es nicht, wenn von einem relativ zu diesem bewegten Bezugskörper aus beurteilt.

Bevor ich in dem Gedankengang fortfahre, muss ich etwas sagen über die Rolle, die der Bezugskörper in der Mechanik Galilei's und Newtons spielt. Überhaupt muss ich bemerken, dass es in der Entwicklung der Wissenschaft nur ein Aufbauen, aber kein Niederreissen gibt. Wenn nicht eine Generation auf das von der früheren Geschichte aufbauen kann, gibt es keine Wissenschaft. Es wäre traurig, wenn die Relativitätstheorie die bisherige Mechanik stürzen müsste, so ähnlich, wie ein tyrannischer Herrscher den andern stürzt. Die Relativitätstheorie ist nichts anderes als ein weiterer Schritt in der Jahrhunderte alten Entwicklung unserer Naturwissenschaft, der die bisher gefundenen Zusammenhänge aufrecht erhält und vertieft und neu hinzufügt. Die Relativitätstheorie stürzt so wenig die Newton'schen und Maxwell'schen Theorien um wie der Völkerbund diejenigen Staaten vernichtet, die ihm beitreten. Sie müssen sich wohl einige Modifikationen ihrer Gesetze gefallen lassen, erlangen aber dafür erhöhte Sphärheit. —

Dem Alltagsleben dient uns die Erde meist als Bezugskörper, dessen einzelne Punkte wiedererkannt werden können. Die mathematische Physik wählt als Bezugskörper (Koordinatensystem) stets von einem Punkt ausgehend, auf einander senkrechte Stäbe. Je der die drei Zahlen (Koordinaten), die durch Messung mit starren Stäben (Massstäben) gewonnen werden. Dabei wird angenommen, dass die Gesetze der Lagerung starrer Körper durch die euklid's Geometrie richtig beschrieben seien. Auf dieser Voraussetzung beruhen alle Ortsangaben der bisherigen Physik. Wo auch ein Punkt gelegen sein mag, immer kann man das Stabsystem und die Messkonstruktionen so vervollständigt denken, dass sie an den betrachteten Punkt heranreichen. Man muss dies so ähnlich denken, wie ein Baugerüst, mit dem man bis zu jedem Türmchen und Schnörkel eines noch so grossen Baues herankommt. Dabei ist in der Physik es gewiss nicht nötig, dass dieses Gerüst wirklich bestehe, wenn man es nur durch indirekte Operationen (mit Lichtstrahlen etc.) konstruiert denken kann.

Die mechanischen Grundgesetze Galileis und Newtons sind nun so beschaffen, dass sie nicht gegenüber beliebig bewegten Bezugskörpern Gültigkeit beanspruchen können, sondern nur gegenüber Bezugskörpern von geeignet gewähltem Bewegungszustand. Man nennt solche in der Mechanik zugelassene Bezugskörper "Inertialsysteme". Es gilt nun in der Mechanik das Gesetz: Ist der Bezugskörper K ein Inertialsystem, so ist auch jeder gegenüber K gleichförmig, gradlinig und drehungsfrei bewegte Bezugskörper ein Inertialsystem. Einfacher gesagt: gelten die mechanischen Gesetze gegen den Erdboden als Bezugskörper, so gelten sie auch gegen gleichförmig fahrenden Eisenbahnwagen als Bezugskörper.

Nun kann ich das vorhin vom Licht Ausgeführte in eine einfache Formel fassen: Relativ zu jedem Inertialsystem gilt - bei richtiger Definition der Zeit - das Satz von der Konstanz der Lichtgeschwindigkeit im leeren Raume. Allgemeiner kann man als den Ausdruck vielfacher Erfahrung den Satz betrachten: Die Naturgesetze sind für alle Inertialsysteme die gleichen. Dieser Satz heisst, speziellles Relativitätsprinzip.

Dass dieser Satz eine neuartige physikalische Forschungsmethode in sich schliesst, kann man folgendermassen auseinander. So gewonnen man habe die Welt bzw. die sie bildenden Einzelereignisse inbezug auf ein Inertialsystem beschrieben, so ist der beobachtete Lalauf von einem anderen Inertialsystem aus betrachtet zwar ein anderer, aber doch vollkommen bekannt. Der allgemeine Regeln ausgerechnet, nach welchem man bei und Zeit

die einzelnen Ereignisse von einem Inertialsystem ins andere
umrechnen kann. Man kann so offenbar nicht nur die
Einzelereignisse umrechnen sondern auch die mathematisch
formulierten Naturgesetze. Das spezielle Relativitätsprinzip
verlangt von diesen, dass sie sich bei jener Umrechnung
nicht ändern. Haben sie diese Eigenschaft nicht, so sind
sie nach dem speziellen Relativitätsprinzip zu verwerfen.
Die Naturgesetze müssen dem speziellen Relativitätsprinzip angepasst
werden.

Bei diesen Untersuchungen zeigte es sich zuerst, dass Newtons
Mechanik einer Modifikation bedarf, wenn es sich um
äusserst rasche Bewegungen handelt, genauer gesagt um Bewegungen, deren Geschwindigkeit gegen die Lichtgeschwindigkeit
nicht verschwindend klein ist. Ferner zeigte es sich, dass die
Trägheit eines Körpers keine ihm eigentümliche Konstante ist,
sondern dass die Trägheit vom Energieinhalt abhängig ist.
Masse und Energie sind wesensgleich.

CONTENTS

EINSTEIN
DECODING THE UNIVERSE

Françoise Balibar

Thames & Hudson

"A man like me arrives at a watershed in his development when he turns from the personal and ephemeral in an effort toward intellectual understanding. What is essential for a man like me is *what* he thinks and *how* he thinks, not what he does or experiences."

Albert Einstein,
Autobiographical Notes, 1946,
translated by Paul A. Schilpp, in
Albert Einstein: Philosopher-Scientist, vol. 1, p. 33

CHAPTER 1
A PASSION TO UNDERSTAND

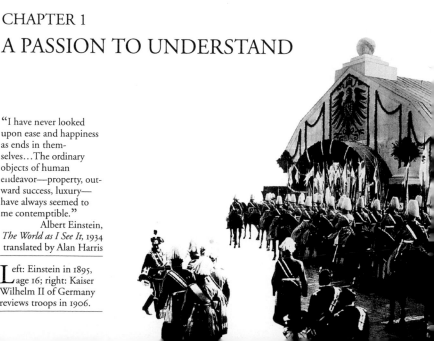

"I have never looked upon ease and happiness as ends in themselves…The ordinary objects of human endeavor—property, outward success, luxury—have always seemed to me contemptible."
Albert Einstein,
The World as I See It, 1934
translated by Alan Harris

Left: Einstein in 1895, age 16; right: Kaiser Wilhelm II of Germany reviews troops in 1906.

Early in 1895, a young man of 16 rode a train from Munich to Milan and reflected on his future. He had just abandoned his studies at the *Gymnasium* (German high school) where his parents had enrolled him and was speeding to Italy to join them. His decision had not been made lightly, for he knew that by missing his upcoming examinations for the baccalaureate degree—which he was assured of passing—he was giving up any chance of attending a university. This action would disappoint and hurt his parents, who had dreamt of a prestigious career for him.

But he could stand it no longer. No reasonable argument could outweigh the disgust he felt for student life. When his parents were still in Munich, he had been able to bear the constraints of a rigid and oppressive educational system. But after some financial reverses, they had moved to Italy, taking their younger daughter, Maja, with them and leaving their son, Albert, in the care of an accommodating family until the end of the academic term.

"Your mere presence here undermines the class's respect for me."—a *Gymnasium* **teacher to Albert Einstein, c. 1894 (recalled by Einstein in a 1940 letter)**

Albert Einstein was born in Germany in 1879. Politically, this was a remarkable period for that country. For centuries there had been no single German state, but only a loose cluster of independent principalities with a

Left: Einstein as a child; and his birth certificate. Right: the main square of Munich in the 19th century.

shared language and a general geographical location, a battlefield for the competing European powers. In less than one generation, by 1871, this patchwork was at last unified under the aegis of Prussia, led by the Prussian statesman Otto von Bismarck. Bismarck was almost the same generation as Einstein's parents; under his leadership, Germany swiftly became a strong and powerful nation, growing rich with rapid industrialization. But prosperity could not entirely conceal persistent religious and regional

"Every sentence he uttered, no matter how routine, he repeated to himself softly."
Maja Winteler-Einstein, "Albert Einstein—A Biographical Sketch," 1924

rifts within the new country, nor cure the severe social problems caused by accelerated industrial growth. An ascendant nationalist and militarist ardor masked these weaknesses enough to allow unification to succeed.

Einstein spent his childhood in the

exciting atmosphere of the new state. Bismarck's
Germany was defined by a taste for power
blended with a glorification of traditional
German culture, philosophy, literature, and
music—a unique mixture of veneration for the
past and idealized modernism. Immanuel Kant,
Johann Wolfgang von Goethe, Friedrich
Schiller, and Ludwig van Beethoven were the
heroes. Institutions of higher learning such as
the *Gymnasium* bred and trained the country's
elite and of course reflected the spirit of the
times, exalting the harmonious development of
the personality as a cultural ideal. Students
followed a rigorous program of study of the
classics and sciences and were held to the
strictest obedience and an almost military discipline.

Above: Einstein, age 14,
with his sister, c. 1893;
below: German troops on
parade, c. 1900. "Within
a good, normal bourgeois
soul there is a vault, which
the master of the house is
proud to show to visitors
and on which is engraved
the word *patriotism.*"

Einstein

Young Einstein could not bear either the
authoritarianism or the forced diet of memorized
encyclopedic data. "It's a true miracle," he commented in
a 1946 memoir, "that modern education hasn't yet
completely smothered the curiosity necessary for
scientific study. For without the required encouragement,
and especially freedom, this fragile plant will wither. It is
a grave mistake to believe that the pleasures of

observation and inquiry can be induced by constraint and a sense of duty."

Exasperated by this militaristic discipline and provoked by the hostility of some his teachers, who could not tolerate his independent mind, Einstein decided to leave for Italy at the end of 1894. He had another compelling reason, which explains even better his refusal to live in Germany in the 1890s: his desire to avoid obligatory military service. By leaving the country before finishing his secondary schooling, he hoped to receive Swiss citizenship and avoid the label of being a deserter. "That a man can take pleasure in marching in fours to the strains of a band is enough to

Einstein, front row, center, at the Munich *Gymnasium,* c. 1890.

make me despise him," he later wrote. "He has only been given his big brain by mistake; a backbone was all he needed."

The emancipation of German Jews at the end of the 19th century

His parents may well have been proud of his bold act. Yet they undoubtedly worried that their son was wasting the very opportunity they had

been denied in their youth: access to those professions that required a university education, with a guarantee of financial security and intellectual satisfaction. Albert's father, Hermann Einstein, had shown some aptitude for mathematics as a youth, but had been forced to abandon the discipline, since in his day universities were barred to a Jew without personal wealth. He had reluctantly gone into business, but had hoped that his son would be able to take advantage of the recently improved status of Jews in Germany.

The rapid economic, social, and political emancipation of the Jews in Bismarck's Germany, and their incredible progress, was one of the great achievements in the history of Europe at the time. In the new state, Jews were

Hermann Einstein (left) graduated from school "with the so-called One-Year-Volunteer Certificate, the possession of which released the young German intelligentsia from the compulsory three years of military service…Hermann Einstein, it seems, showed a marked inclination for mathematics, and would have liked to pursue studies in this or some related field. His father's means, however, with a large family to maintain and two daughters to provide for, were too limited to allow Hermann to pursue his inclination. As a result, he decided to become a merchant. Perhaps this very potential, left fallow in the father, developed all the more strongly in his son Albert."

Maja Winteler-Einstein, "Albert Einstein— A Biographical Sketch," 1924

granted full citizenship. The emptying of the ghettos was a slow but irreversible process that had begun at the end of the 18th century with the dissemination of ideas from the French Revolution. Gradually these led to local statutes granting partial emancipation, which became total and definitive in 1869. Born ten years later, Albert Einstein belonged to the first generation of German Jews whose civic rights had been granted by law from birth.

At the same time, the spread of capitalism in Germany that accompanied its political unification was spectacularly promising. German Jews, who, unlike the old privileged class, had nothing to lose, actively participated in this expansion and quickly rose to prominent economic positions. This social advancement was often marked by a desire for cultural assimilation.

Einstein's parents were part of this contemporary trend. Nonpracticing Jews, they were probably convinced that antisemitism would soon become a shameful memory and that German Jews would be

Left: Pauline Einstein, Albert's mother. "The financial means brought to the marriage by his wife, and the progress of the business, might have allowed his young family not just a carefree but a very prosperous life…Had Hermann remained in Ulm, his son Albert would also have been granted a more carefree youth… Einstein's mother…possessed a sound native wit. Her feelings were seldom given free rein and, although accustomed from childhood to wealthy surroundings, she adjusted— with difficulty, but with understanding—to her altered circumstances. Married at 17, she learned early about the realities of life,"
Maja Winteler-Einstein, "Albert Einstein— A Biographical Sketch," 1924

Below: the Marienplatz, Munich's main square, in the late 19th century.

Germans like any others. Not surprisingly, they wanted their son to have a middle-class profession. The opportunities for young Jewish men to enjoy social success had never been greater than at the end of the 19th century. Unfortunately, Albert's generation did not reap the fruits of this hope, but rather experienced the resurgence of antisemitism in the 1930s, then fascism, and exile or death in concentration camps.

Businessman father, inventor uncle

Not only for Jews, but in general, the 1890s were a time of economic boom in Germany, particularly in Bavaria, where the Einstein family lived. Hermann's brother Jakob was the personification of the new spirit of enterprise. An electrical engineer, he had designed a dynamo as well as electrical gauges and meters. He held several patents and wanted to market his inventions commercially. Germany was in the forefront of the move to provide electricity to homes, industries, and city streets. The incandescent lightbulb, invented by Thomas Edison in 1879, was becoming a fixture in every house and business and quickly turning into the greatest consumer of electricity. Together, Jakob and Hermann redirected their efforts to setting up a business in 1885.

Unfortunately the effort was only a partial success. In 1893 the firm failed to win an important contract and had to be closed. Then Jakob had a good idea: since electrification was already well established in Germany, it would be better to try their luck in Italy, where the process was just beginning. The entire family picked up and left for northern Italy, going first to Milan, then Pavia, and leaving Albert to finish his schooling in Munich.

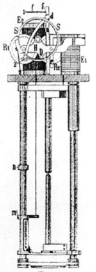

Fig. 1.

Fig. 2.

"A younger brother of Hermann Einstein, named Jakob, who later exerted a certain intellectual influence on Albert while he was growing up, finished his studies in engineering and wanted to start a plumbing and electrical business in Munich...His fertile imagination and manifold ideas led him, among other things, to construct a dynamo of his own invention."

Maja Winteler-Einstein,
"Albert Einstein—
A Biographical Sketch,"
1924

Left: Jakob Einstein's designs for a dynamo and an arc lamp; above: the Einstein electrical-supply factory in Pavia, Italy, c. 1900.

1907: Einstein enrolls in the Polytechnic Institute of Zurich

Hermann Einstein's career in the electrical industry played an essential role in the life of his son. Indeed, since Albert had grown up in a technical and industrial milieu, it seemed natural, after he abandoned his chance

"To be a good student at the Polytechnic, one has to understand easily, to be able to concentrate one's energies on the material presented, and to like order…A healthy and independent mind was

prized above breadth of knowledge. In the eyes of students, a professor was not an authority figure but a man with a distinct personality."

Albert Einstein

to get into a university, to enroll in one of the great engineering schools. The Polytechnic Institute of Zurich, or *Polytechnikum,* was a prestigious institution that prepared students for university-level teaching careers. This school seemed to Albert the best place to develop his aptitude and predilection for mathematics and to satisfy the career aspirations of his parents. A further advantage was that it did not require the baccalaureate degree from a German high school, since one gained admission through an examination. He took the entrance examination as an independent candidate in the fall of 1895. He was still one year younger than the minimum age, but obtained a dispensation. Though he failed the exam, he was not discouraged, but enrolled for the next semester in a school that specialized in helping students prepare for the entrance exam. The following year he passed and entered the Polytechnic.

There he met Mileva Marić, a young woman of Serbian parentage who was, like him, a mathematics and physics student. It is difficult today to appreciate fully the significance of a woman becoming a student at this celebrated school at that period. The Polytechnic was well ahead of its time in its policies regarding the education of women. In fact, it was the one of the first institutions of higher learning in Europe to open its doors to women.

Albert and Mileva fell in love and soon decided to set up household together. For Einstein's family there was no question of his marrying a foreigner who was not Jewish. To make matters worse, the career Mileva was pursuing was hardly considered feminine, she was lame, and she was three years older than Albert. He had terrible scenes with his parents, who were already strapped financially and who accused him of wanting their death. Though deeply angry, Einstein gave in. In 1901 Mileva realized that she was pregnant and returned to her family to give birth to a daughter in 1902. All traces of this child quickly disappeared, and it is likely that she died very young. Returning to Zurich, Mileva failed her final exams at the Polytechnic and found herself without degree or profession.

Mileva Marić was among those young women from Eastern Europe who came to the West to study. Her life was more emancipated than that of her middle-class contemporaries in the West, who could only attend colleges for women. The daughter of a Serb bureaucrat in the Austro-Hungarian Empire, she was singled out by her teachers and sent to finish her studies, first in a boys' high school and later in Heidelberg, Germany. She enrolled in the Polytechnic in the same year as Einstein and was the only woman in the class. Above: Mileva was 21 in 1896, when she came to Zurich to study.

Opposite above: the Polytechnic of Zurich, near the train station; below: Einstein as a student in Aarau, c. 1895–96.

The Bern patent office

The early years of Einstein's adulthood were not particularly happy. It is true that in July 1900 he received his degree from one of the most prestigious schools in Europe. But he was greatly disappointed to learn that he was not going to be offered a position as assistant professor at the university, as he had been led to expect. This may have been due to problems he had had with one of his professors in Zurich, or, as Mileva thought, to antisemitism. For two years he toiled at minor trades, the most onerous of which was private tutoring. In June 1902, thanks to a recommendation from a school friend's father in Zurich, he at last obtained a settled position as a specialist in the Swiss patent office in Bern. By this time he had become a Swiss citizen.

Much has been written about the fact that this great genius had to work in a job so far beneath his ability. But Einstein himself always maintained that in a university position he would have been preoccupied with preparing courses and worrying about the promotion track, and far less free to think. Working in the patent office suited him perfectly: he had to appraise inventions, usually electrical, for which he had a real aptitude, and at night he could contemplate the great questions of physics at his leisure.

Nonetheless, it would be wrong to characterize the period of 1899–1905

"For me it was a real blessing to work on the final wording of patents. Jobs [like this one] are such that anyone of average intelligence can meet their obligations. Your daily routine is not subject to the vagaries of inspiration, and you needn't live in fear of seeing your efforts come to nothing."

Albert Einstein

Below left: Einstein in the patent office in Bern, 1902.

Privatstunden in

Mathematik u. Physik

erende und Schüler erteilt grünblichst

nstein, Inhaber des eidgen.

t. Fachlehrerdiploms,

"During his student years Einstein formed a close friendship with [his] classmate Marcel Grossmann. Each week they went together to the Cafe Metropol on the Limatquai in Zurich. He once made a remark that is so charming and characteristic that I cannot resist quoting it here: 'I concede [said Grossmann] that I did after all gain something rather important from the study of physics. Before, when I sat on a chair and felt the trace of heat left by my "pre-sitter," I used to shudder a little. That is completely gone, for on this point physics has taught me that heat is something completely impersonal.'"

Banesh Hoffmann,
Albert Einstein: Creator and Rebel, 1972

Above left: Marcel Grossmann, Albert Einstein, Gustav Geissler, and Eugen Grossmann near Zurich in 1899; near left: an advertisement placed by Einstein in a Bern newspaper in 1902, offering private tutoring in mathematics and physics.

as happy. Einstein had simultaneously to face unemployment, the loss of a child, and the failure of Mileva's professional life, not to mention the incessant harassment of his parents, which ended only with the death of Hermann Einstein in 1902. He was then finally able to marry Mileva.

Thought as refuge

And yet, during this time Einstein was incubating and developing the stunning revelations of 1905. He himself said more than once that it was the chance to use his mind that gave him the strength to bear his troubles.

Writing his autobiography at the age of 67, at the request of an American publisher, Einstein related that he was "by nature precocious" and was aware at a young age "of the vanity of hopes and ambitions which propel most people into the whirlwinds of a frantic life."

Recalling his youth, Einstein wrote in 1953: "To the immortal Olympia Academy! In your short active life, dear Academy, you took delight, with childlike joy, in all that was clear and intelligent. Your members created you to make fun of your long-established sister Academies." Top: the Cafe Metropol in Zurich at the turn of the century; above: Conrad Habicht, Maurice Solovine, and Einstein, founders of the "Olympia Academy." Solovine had answered Einstein's advertisement.

By his own account, even as a child he had seen the world as cruel and hypocritical. At one time in his early youth he found refuge in strict religious observance. But he soon abandoned religion, he said, after reading works of popular science that convinced him that the Bible could not be true. Commenting on this religious phase of his life, he added, "It seemed clear to me that the loss of my childhood's devout paradise was the first attempt to liberate myself from the bonds of an entirely personal universe and an existence dominated by desires, hopes, and primitive feelings."

All his life Einstein sought shelter from the unbearable cruelty of the world and tried to free himself from a life governed by feelings that he considered base. Science proved a bastion: in seeking the solution to the enigma posed by "the vast world that exists independently of men" he escaped the limitations of the material existence. "The contemplation of the world was like the promise of a liberation," he wrote in a 1946 autobiography.

He sometimes maintained that only the pleasure of thought allowed him to find true liberty. He had a saying, or motto, reminiscent of the title of the great Schiller poem that became the chorus in Beethoven's Ninth Symphony, but which might also be considered a key to his success, or what is called his genius: "die Freude am Denken," the joy of thought.

Einstein apparently had few natural paternal instincts. With Mileva he had two sons, Hans Albert, born in 1904, and Eduard, born in 1910. Eduard was chronically ill and later developed schizophrenia. After their divorce in 1919, Einstein left Mileva to care for the children, providing for them financially. His relations with his elder son, Hans Albert, remained chilly until quite late in life. Below: Albert, Mileva, and Hans Albert, soon after the boy's birth in 1904.

"The most fascinating subject at the time that I was a student was Maxwell's theory. What made this theory appear revolutionary was the transition from [Newton's] forces at a distance to fields as fundamental variables. The incorporation of optics into the theory of electromagnetism… was like a revelation."

Albert Einstein,
Autobiographical Notes, 1946,
translated by Paul A. Schilpp, in
Albert Einstein: Philosopher-Scientist, vol. 1, p. 33

CHAPTER 2
PHYSICS IN CRISIS

"The special relativity theory, which was simply a systematic extension of the electrodynamics of Maxwell and Lorentz, had consequences which reached beyond itself."
Albert Einstein,
letter to *The Times*
(London),
November 28, 1919

Left: Einstein at 14; right: James Clerk Maxwell, c. 1870.

A house on the verge of collapse

When Einstein set out on his scientific career in the first years of the 20th century, physics was in crisis. Research in the 19th century still relied upon Isaac Newton's 17th-century theories. Groundbreaking work by the Scottish physicist James Clerk Maxwell (1831–79) and others led to the radical rethinking and redefinition of two disciplines: mechanics, the science of the motion of material objects; and electromagnetism, the science of the motion of radiant energy, or waves, including light, X-rays, and other radiation.

Unfortunately, the theories governing these two branches of science contradicted one another on numerous points. Einstein compared physics at the time to a house built in two parts, one added to the other causing tensions and fissures within the masonry. These fissures were so serious and so wide that many of science's "architects" called for demolition of one or the other and reconstruction on a more secure foundation. To some physicists this scientific debate became a personal drama; Ludwig Boltzmann (1844–1906), the founder of statistical mechanics, took his own life in 1906, partly because he saw no way out of a conflict that he thought had paralyzed his thinking.

The principle of relativity

Mechanics, the science founded by Galileo (1564–1642) and greatly expanded by Newton (1642–1727), set out to

Newton's work on the theory of gravitation provided scientists with a model of the physical laws of the universe that endured nearly intact for 200 years. Gravitation, together with the three laws of dynamics he described in his *Principia Mathematica (Mathematical Principles of Natural Philosophy)*, dictated his understanding of the movements of the planets. Right: the title page of the *Principia*, 1687.

A stone dropped from the top of the mast of a ship falls straight, in line with the mast. The result of the experiment is the same whether the ship is in motion or at dock: either way, the stone falls to the foot of the mast, although one might at first suppose that it would land toward the back of the ship when the ship is in motion. This demonstrates the principle of relativity. To a sailor perched on top of the mast, who is moving along with the ship in the same straight line, the stone's path is a straight line downward. But to an observer on shore the stone's path describes a curve, called a parabola.

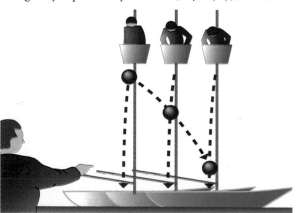

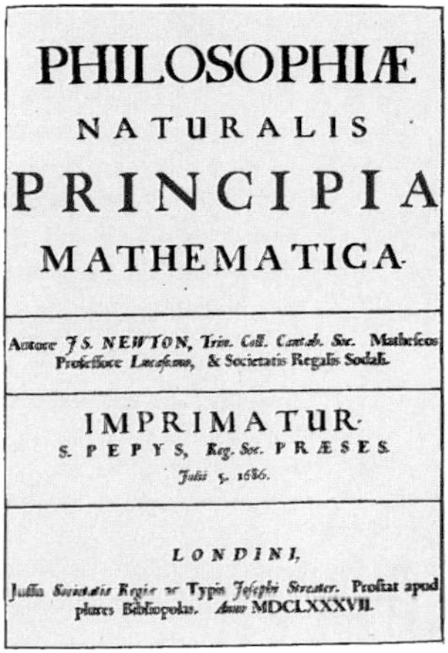

PHILOSOPHIÆ
NATURALIS
PRINCIPIA
MATHEMATICA.

Autore *J. S. NEWTON*, *Trin. Coll. Cantab. Soc.* Matheseos Professore *Lucasiano*, & Societatis Regalis Sodali.

IMPRIMATUR.
S. PEPYS, *Reg. Soc.* PRÆSES.
Julii 5. 1686.

LONDINI,
Jussu Societatis Regiæ ac Typis *Josephi Streater*. Prostat apud plures Bibliopolas. *Anno* MDCLXXXVII.

Axiomata
sive
Leges Motûs

Lex I.

Corpus omne perseverare in statu suo quiescendi vel movendi uniformiter in directum, nisi quatenus a viribus impressis cogitur statum illum mutare.

Projectilia perseverant in motibus suis nisi quatenus a resistentia aeris retardantur et vi gravitatis impelluntur deorsum. Trochus, cujus partes cohaerendo perpetuo retrahunt sese a motibus rectilineis, non cessat rotari nisi quatenus ab aere retardatur. Majora autem Planetarum et Cometarum corpora motus suos et progressivos et circulares in spatiis minus resistentibus factos conservant diutius.

Lex II.

Mutationem motus proportionalem esse vi motrici impressae et fieri secundum lineam rectam qua vis illa imprimitur.

Si vis aliqua motum quemvis generet, vis dupla duplum, tripla triplum generabit, sive simul et semel, sive gradatim et successive impressa fuerit. Et hic motus quoniam in eandem semper plagam cum vi generatrice determinatur, si corpus antea movebatur, motui ejus vel conspiranti additur, vel contrario subducitur, vel obliquo oblique adjicitur et cum eo secundum utriusque determinationem componitur.

Lex III.

Actioni contrariam semper et aequalem esse reactionem: sive corporum duorum actiones in se mutuo semper esse aequales et in partes contrarias dirigi.

Quicquid premit vel trahit alterum tantundem ab eo premitur vel trahitur. Siquis lapidem digito premit, premitur et hujus digitus a lapide. Si equus lapidem funi allegatum trahit, retrahetur etiam et equus aequaliter in lapidem: nam funis utrinque distentus eodem relaxandi se conatu urgebit equum versus lapidem, ac lapidem versus equum, tantumque impediet progressum unius quantum promovet progressum alterius. Si corpus aliquod in corpus aliud impingens, motum ejus vi sua quomodocunque mutaverit, idem quoque vicissim in motu proprio eandem mutationem in partem contrariam vi alterius (ob aequalitatem pressionis mutuae) subibit. His actionibus aequales

Above: the three laws of motion enunciated by Newton (in Latin) in his manuscript for the *Principia Mathematica.*

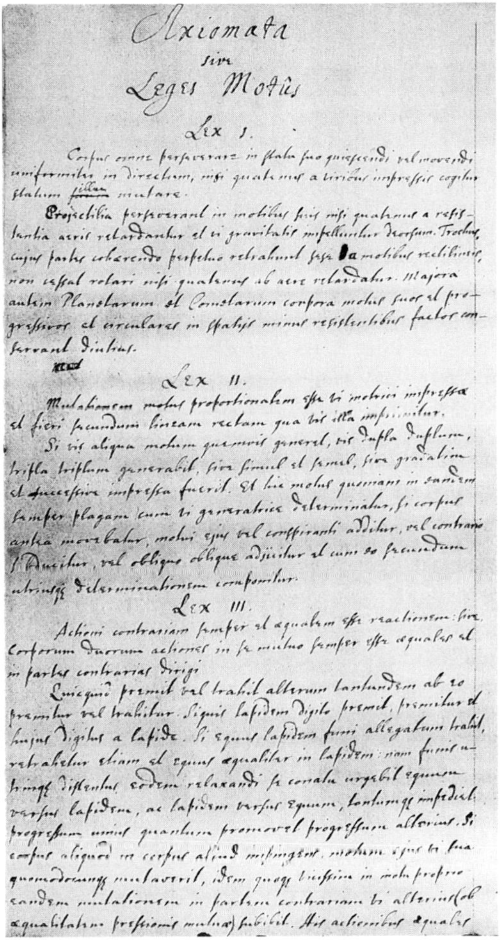

describe the motion of bodies, whether a grain of dust dancing in a cloud of smoke or a planet revolving around the sun. This science deals with material objects, that is, objects comprising a defined quantity of matter. Mechanics is based on the principle of relativity, expressed for the first time not by Einstein (as is often believed), but by Galileo. This principle governs all laws of mechanics, in particular Newton's three laws of dynamics (the forces that govern the motion of matter).

The principle of relativity states that the same physical laws apply—that is, things occur in the same manner—whether they are observed in a stationary state or within a moving context. For example, an object will fall in the same direction and at the same rate on land or on a sailing ship (to use Galileo's example). So if we observe only what occurs inside the cabin, it is impossible to know if we are in a ship in full sail or one in drydock on the ground. This is true, at

TRAITE
DE LA LVMIERE.

Où font expliquées

Les caufes de ce qui luy arrive

Dans la REFLEXION, & dans la REFRACTION.

least as long as the ship moves at a constant speed and in a straight line. As Galileo put it, the movement of the vehicle is "as nothing"; it does not count, since it is not "felt."

The absence of sensation therefore is no proof that one is immobile. Without perceiving it, we may very well be propelled in a motion at constant speed and in a straight line. A passenger seated in an airplane is immobile in relation to the walls of the vehicle but mobile in relation to the earth, which itself is in motion with respect to the sun, which in turn undergoes a certain movement within our galaxy; and the galaxy itself is also in motion, and so on. In short, nothing exists in a state of absolute immobility;

The Dutch mathematician Christian Huygens (1629–95) formulated an early version of wave theory, in opposition to Newton's theory of mechanics: "When we see a luminous object, [its light] does not reach us as a substance traveling as a bullet or an arrow passes through the air." Rather, light emanates outward from the source, moving in an expanding sphere of waves, with each point on the front of the wave behaving like a new source of radiation. "Thus, in the flame of a candle, with the points A, B, C distinguished, the concentric circles described around these points represent the waves that come from them." Left: the title page and a diagram from the 1690 French edition of his "Treatise on Light."

everything is in motion relative to something else. (The exception, as we shall see, is light, which moves at the same speed from all points of view.)

The first stumbling block: Maxwell's ether

Maxwell had studied how electric and magnetic forces influence one another, developing the theory of electromagnetism in the 1850s to describe the properties and action of light and heat, in mathematical terms, as waves. A wave is different from an object or body of matter; it is something that is propagated, from point to point, in the manner of water rippling outward on the surface of a pond into which a stone has been dropped. When the ripple travels from one side of the pond to the other, the water itself does not move across the pond. Light waves are not propagated in water, however, but in space. Maxwell thought that they were propagated in something he called the "ether."

Left: Trinity College, in Cambridge, England, is one of the memorable places in the history of physics. Newton studied there from 1660 to 1665, and then taught there for another twenty years. Today, an apple tree marks the location of a small building in which he carried out alchemical experiments and which caught fire under strange circumstances. A century and a half later, in 1850, James Clerk Maxwell was also affiliated with Trinity College as a student.

Maxwell tried all his life to explain the propagation of light as a mechanical phenomenon, using models with gears and toothed wheels. The model below was built by Charles Wheatstone, one of his disciples.

According to Maxwell, we must imagine that the world is filled in every nook and cranny with a medium, the ether, whose existence is necessary for the propagation of light. But what is this ether made of? What does it look like—water, air, glass? Is it heavy, liquid, solid, elastic? Maxwell's theory gives a few vague responses: the ether is "no doubt" colorless, "probably" weightless—something like gelatin. Over time he stripped his concept of all physical properties, leaving it with one characteristic alone: an absolute immobility. This immediately placed it in direct contradiction to the principle of relativity.

Maxwell's theory of light waves caused a fissure in the fine structure erected by Newton and his successors. In physics a principle allows no exceptions; otherwise it must be abandoned. At the beginning of the 20th century, therefore, physicists became embroiled in a

Maxwell believed that to explore new phenomena, for whose description there are neither concepts nor even words, one must reason by analogy. He saw the propagation of light as analogous to the generation of movement in a material space—the ether. He did not claim to know the composition of the ether, but described patterns to approximate it. Left: a diagram of Maxwell's concept of the flow of light through ether. The ether is compartmentalized into cells that touch one another while rotating, thus transmitting a motion from one point of the ether to another.

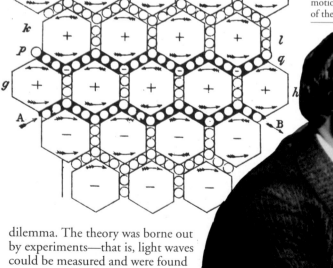

dilemma. The theory was borne out by experiments—that is, light waves could be measured and were found to behave as the theory predicted. So either light was propagated in an immobile ether, and the relativity principle must be abandoned, or the sacrosanct principle of relativity must be preserved and the ether could not exist. But in that case, how could the propagation of light be explained? Either the mechanics wing of the building, or the other wing, electromagnetism, must be destroyed, it seemed.

The second stumbling block: continuity versus discontinuity

Adding to the confusion, a contradiction of a more philosophical nature also tormented physicists: how to reconcile two opposites, continuity and discontinuity.

In 1900 many physicists already believed what we know today: that matter is made up of atoms, small particles that combine in various ways. The movements and behavior of atoms are described by the science of mechanics. Like grains of sand, they can be separated from one another and counted one by one—at least in theory, for they are extremely numerous. Examined at the atomic level, the spaces between atoms appear to be empty "holes,"

If the ether exists and is absolutely immobile, the speed of light traveling through it on the surface of the earth ought to be different when the light is propagated in the direction of the motion of the earth (that is, flowing with the ether) and when it goes in the reverse direction (against the ether). The American physicists Albert A. Michelson (1852–1931) and E. W. Morley (1838–1923) devised an experiment to demonstrate this difference. To their surprise, the result proved negative: the speed of light was the same in both directions—invalidating the hypothesis that light traveled in an ether. Left: two images of light broken into its spectrum.

Far left: Michelson working at a microscope, c. 1910.

which suggests that matter is discontinuous—another way of saying that it is not solid.

Continuity and discontinuity are two totally opposite qualities; a thing cannot be both discontinuous and continuous, or change from a continuous to a discontinuous state. At the most it is possible to make false continuity from discontinuity, just as sand may appear continuous when viewed from above, although it is not.

What about light? Is it discontinuous or continuous? It seems to be continuous, since it contains no "holes" and moves in continuous waves, but might that be a false appearance? Maxwell's experiments and mathematical equations showed that light must be described as truly continuous and not as a false continuity.

Thus matter is discontinuous, while light is continuous. At first glance, the necessity to define them as opposites seems logical enough. After all, one has weight and the other has none; one is generally opaque, the other invisible,

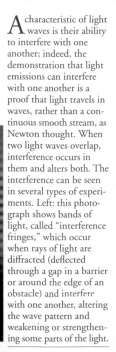

A molecule of platinum photographed with a field-effect microscope.

A characteristic of light waves is their ability to interfere with one another; indeed, the demonstration that light emissions can interfere with one another is a proof that light travels in waves, rather than a continuous smooth stream, as Newton thought. When two light waves overlap, interference occurs in them and alters both. The interference can be seen in several types of experiments. Left: this photograph shows bands of light, called "interference fringes," which occur when rays of light are diffracted (deflected through a gap in a barrier or around the edge of an obstacle) and interfere with one another, altering the wave pattern and weakening or strengthening some parts of the light.

and so on. Granted, but the physicist must also bear in mind that light and matter are not unrelated. To begin with, light is born of matter; we can generate light when we heat oil in an old lamp or the copper wire filament of an incandescent lightbulb, or when we "excite" a gas with the help of an electrical charge, as in a neon light.

How is it conceivable that discontinuous matter can be transformed into continuous waves? Here again, it is difficult to reconcile the atomic theory of matter, based on mechanics, with the theory of light. This was the first problem that Einstein faced.

Below: the filament of an incandescent lightbulb and its riddle: how can matter, which is discontinuous, produce light, which is continuous?

"I promise you four papers…, the first of which I might send you soon…The paper deals with radiation and the energy properties of light and is very revolutionary…The fourth paper is only a rough draft at this point, and is an electrodynamics of moving bodies which employs a modification of the theory of space and time."

Letter from Albert Einstein
to Conrad Habicht, spring 1905,
translated by Anna Beck

CHAPTER 3
A YEAR OF MIRACLES

Left: Einstein in Zurich, 1912. Right: among the discoveries of 1905, he is best remembered for the famous equation for the relationship between mass and energy.

$$E = Mc^2.$$

A problem well stated is a problem half solved

1905 was a year of extraordinary achievements. Within the space of six months, Einstein published a series of important papers that unraveled the tangle of contradictions plaguing physics. In March he demonstrated that the perceived opposition between continuity and discontinuity does not exist, for both light and matter are composed of particles. This was called the quantum hypothesis of light. (A "quantum" is a fixed quantity of something; the word is often used to describe particles.) In June he presented a theory of light, called the special theory of

ANNALEN

DER

PHYSIK

BEGRÜNDET UND FORTGEFÜHRT DURCH

F. A. C. GREN, L. W. GILBERT, J. C. POGGENDORFF, G. UND E. WIEDEMANN

VIERTE FOLGE.

BAND 17.   HEFT 5.

DER GANZEN REIHE 322, BANDES 5. HEFT.

KURATORIUM:

F. KOHLRAUSCH, M. PLANCK, G. QI
W. C. RÖNTGEN, E. WARBUR

UNTER MITWIRKUNG

DER DEUTSCHEN PHYSIKALISCHEN GE

relativity, that dispensed with the idea that light must travel through a medium such as an ether, thus bridging the gap between mechanics and electromagnetism. He also explained the photoelectric effect, a phenomenon that had been observed— but not fully understood—in which metal, when struck by electromagnetic radiation (such as light) emits electrons (negatively charged particles within an

Left: the title page of the 1906 issue of *Annals of Physics,* in which Einstein's revolutionary paper was published. Below: Max Planck, a crucial figure in German science, was on the editorial board of the journal. Planck suffered a tragic fate: in 1914 he signed an appeal in favor of World War I, then just beginning, which he came to regret bitterly. Two of his children died in it. Later, though hostile to Nazism, he went along with the regime in the hope of saving the research institutions he had created, and did not protest when Jewish colleagues were persecuted.

Left: the most productive period of Einstein's life coincided with his term of employment in the Swiss patent office in Bern.

Inscribed on the grave of the physicist Ludwig Boltzmann in Vienna is the formula that bears his name: $S = k \log W$, where S is entropy and W is the corresponding probability. Einstein used this equation in a new way in 1905; it helped him to discover the granular (discontinuous, or quantum) nature of light.

"I am truly a 'lone traveler' and have never belonged to my country, my home, my friends, or even my immediate family, with my whole heart; in the face of all these ties, I have never lost a sense of distance and a need for solitude—feelings which increase with the years."

Albert Einstein, 1930, in *The World as I See It*, 1934, translated by Alan Harris

atom). And he presented his great discovery that (under certain circumstances) the speed of light is constant for all observers in differing contexts.

Before we explore these theories in more detail, we should pay tribute to the German physics establishment of the time, particularly the publishers of the leading physics journal *Annalen der Physik* (*Annals of Physics*), who took the risk—one that few journals today would dare—of publishing two revolutionary articles written by an unknown employee of the Swiss patent office. Apparently the German university, an institution otherwise all too rigid and hierarchical, was not above allowing a marginal figure to speak his mind. And we should also not overlook the young Einstein's remarkable mental balance. It's easy to imagine how destabilizing it might have been for a young man of 26, working alone, to come up with the solution to problems that had foiled people with twice his experience for generations. Yet he did so with astonishing ease.

March 1905: the discovery of light quanta

As a preamble to his first article, Einstein issued a diagnosis of the problem: physics would remain stalled until it could get past the opposition between continuity and discontinuity, a traditional stumbling block that had long made it impossible to explain with any accuracy how light is produced by matter. He then analyzed how light is produced, beginning with the emission of light by a body that is heated, and explaining how light knocks electrons out of a metal body (the photoelectric effect). This built upon the discoveries made in 1900 by the German physicist Max Planck (1858–1947), who had described how heated metal radiates light—why it glows—and who had first formulated the "quantum" concept as a means of measuring this radiant energy.

Maxwell had seen energy as central to the understanding of the physical properties and behavior of both light and matter. Planck had then studied the way the energy of heated matter is transformed into light energy. Einstein's March 1905 paper reconciled Maxwell's wave concept of light and Planck's quantum concept of energy. He noticed that the transformation of light was understandable only if one supposed that light was made up of "grains," or "atoms of energy," which he called light quanta. Today, light quanta are known as photons; they are the basic unit of light and all other forms of electromagnetic radiation (such as X-rays, microwaves, and radio waves).

Einstein was a convinced atomist; he belonged to a generation that, even if it had never yet seen atoms, believed firmly in their existence. Even more, he was an ardent defender of statistical mechanics. This discipline studies the motion of atoms according to Newton's laws of mechanics, concentrating not on their individual movements but on the total effect of atomic motions, or their statistical average—a viewpoint justified by the enormous number of atoms contained in even a single gram of matter.

The iridescent colors that appear on the surface of a soap bubble can be explained only through the continuous-wave theory of light. When white light strikes the transparent film of a soap bubble, some reflects off the top surface of the film and some passes through and bounces off the bottom surface of the film and back up. The two sets of light waves interfere with one another. The light that finally emerges has a color that depends on the thickness of the soap film, since the thickness causes different wavelengths (colors) to interfere. Above: an enlarged detail of the surface of a thin film of soapy water.

Continuity and discontinuity of light

The energy of both light and matter is discontinuous, he said, made up of particles. Must we conclude then that light itself, like matter, also has a discontinuous structure that only appears to be continuous? Einstein considered the problem innovatively, and thought—rightly, as it turned out—that light had properties of both continuity and discontinuity. The discontinuity of light is suggested by the hypothesis of light quanta (called photons), while its

The neon lights of Broadway illustrate the discontinuous property of light. Each colored tube contains atoms of just one kind of gas: atoms of neon, rubidium, and so on. When these atoms are electrically excited, they emit particles of light that bear a clearly defined energy, in

continuous quality is required by Maxwell's theory, which was so admirably verified by numerous experiments. It remained to be explained why light manifests its continuous properties in certain circumstances and its discontinuous aspect in others. For instance, a rainbow is formed by the refraction of light within millions of raindrops, and refrac-

conformity with the quantum hypothesis.

tion is a wave phenomenon. But the filament of an incandescent lightbulb produces light in a flow of discontinuous particles, as Planck had discovered. Thus, light is neither continuous nor discontinuous, or rather, it is both, depending on what features the experiment is designed to see.

The problem was thus not totally resolved, and Einstein in 1905 would have been hard pressed to answer the question: What is light made of? Nevertheless, one point had clearly been confirmed: light was not just a continuous wave; it also had atomic, discontinuous properties. Einstein had discovered an object, light, that resisted the continuity/discontinuity

"I could have gotten a sound mathematical education, but I worked most of the time in the physics laboratory; I was fascinated by the direct contact with experience." Einstein was not the pure theoretician that people assumed him to be. He devoted a lot of time to building a machine designed to measure small quantities of electricity in the atmosphere. Below: Einstein's laboratory at the Zurich Polytechnic.

dichotomy; at the same time, he had shown that the theories of light and of matter were compatible.

Thrilled as he was at having found even a partial solution to the problems that had plagued physicists of the preceding generation, Einstein could not foresee that this question of the true nature of light—of the "reality" of light quanta—would haunt him all his life.

June 1905: the theory of relativity

"The introduction of a 'light ether' will prove superfluous," a triumphant Einstein announced in the first paragraph of his June 1905 article. Thus he dismissed the second contradiction that had troubled physical theory.

But how was it possible to dispense with the ether, which according to Maxwell was the medium whose wavelike vibrations made up light itself? Einstein declared that light is simply not produced

by a field being set in motion—neither the ether nor some other medium.

How, then, could light be defined? Einstein began by accepting one of the conclusions of Maxwell's theory: namely, that light, however the person observing it may be moving, must always move at a given speed c, that is, approximately 186,000 miles per second (299,460 km per second). If light is conceived of as the motion of a wave in an immobile ether, this conclusion contradicts the principle of relativity, because the speed of this wave ought to depend on the speed (in relation to the ether) of the person observing it. Einstein's genius was in abolishing this contradiction by suppressing the very idea that light is the motion of a wave in the ether.

Why should the constancy of the speed of light be in contradiction with the relativity principle? This was the question Einstein asked himself in 1904. "I knew that the principle of the constant speed of light was in conflict with the rule of addition of velocities [the relativity postulate] we knew of well in mechanics, and I found it difficult to resolve the question why the two cases were in conflict with each other," he recalled in 1922. "That was a very beautiful day when I visited [a friend]…Discussing the matter with him, I suddenly comprehended it…My solution was really the very concept of time—that is, that time is not absolutely defined…Five weeks after my recognition of this, the present theory of special relativity was completed." Left: a receipt signed by Einstein for lessons he gave in electrical engineering in Switzerland in 1905: "Received for 4 lessons in electricity, from 24 October to 21 November '05. 18 francs, Einstein."

Light, according to Einstein, is uniquely defined by the fact that it always moves at speed c for all observers.

Imagine that the ether does not exist; and let us abandon the idea that light is a vibration of this field that is propagated from one portion to the next. Is it possible to rebuild physics on this basis? Must we preserve the principle of relativity? Yes, says Einstein. In fact, nothing now stands in the way of this principle. This leads to his conclusion: light, too, obeys the principle of relativity. This fundamental principle, which until then had been valid only for mechanics, now governs both matter and light and allows no exceptions.

Thus he sets out to construct a theory resting on two principles: the "principle of light"—light always (regardless of the motion of the observer) moves at speed c—and the principle of relativity—nothing can be absolutely immobile.

The resulting theory is called the theory of relativity for the very reason that it combines under the scope of the relativity principle both the theory of matter and the theory of light.

It has often been pointed out that this name is not ideal. To tell the truth, the theory of relativity is a theory of *in*variables; it seeks out whatever in nature does *not* vary, regardless of the observer's vantage point. The constant c, the speed of light, is a good example of an invariable—something that is not relative.

The simultaneity in question

The unification of the theories of light and of matter led to an unexpected change in our intuitive ideas about space and time. Einstein begins by demonstrating a paradoxical fact: a passenger in a train experiences two events as

This amusing note in an unidentiied hand reads: "Short definition of Relativity: there is no hitching post in the Universe—so far as we know." The smaller notation, in German, is in Einstein's hand: "Read and found correct, A. Einstein." One could quarrel with the disclaimer "so far as we know," since relativity does not depend on some knowledge that is subject to rebuttal; rather, it is a principle on which physical theory is based.

hort definition of

There is no hitchi in the Universe as we know

gelesen und richtig befunden A. Einstein

Put another way, there exists no privileged vantage point for viewing the world.

simultaneous, but these same two events are not simultaneous for an individual who is on the ground, watching the train pass by. This observer sees one of the events occur before the other.

Let us imagine the following situation: two persons, seated at opposite ends of a train car that is moving from left to right, take a photograph with a flash camera. A passenger seated in the middle of the car (called A) perceives the two flashes at the same time. For him, the two photographers at the opposite ends of the car pushed their flash buttons at the same instant. But to an individual (called B) who is watching the train go by, observer A, seated in the middle of the car, is moving toward the right—with the train—and is thus advancing to meet the light emitted by the flash bulb of the photographer situated at the front of the car, whereas he is "fleeing" ahead of the light emitted by the photographer at the rear of the car. But by virtue of the principle posited by Einstein, light always arrives at speed c at the eye of observer A, whether it comes from the left or the right, whether he is moving away from or toward the light. Now the distance that must be covered by the light emitted at the right to reach observer A (who is moving toward the light) is smaller than the distance to be covered by the light emitted at the left to reach the same observer A, who is fleeing from it. Since light always moves at velocity c, the time taken by the light at the right to reach the eye of observer A is shorter than the time required by the light at the left to reach the same observer.

Thus, for B, the two flashes were not set off at the same instant. Who is correct? A or B? Both, according to Einstein. Contrary to what ordinary intuition suggests, two simultaneous events for A are not simultaneous for B, who does not share in A's motion. This is a very awkward

In the sixth line of this manuscript by Einstein concerning the "general relationship between mass and energy $(E = Mc^2)$," the author cites the German mathematician and philosopher Gottfried Wilhelm von Leibniz (1646–1716). From an early age—perhaps more than in later life—Einstein was interested in philosophical questions. As a boy of 13 he had been much influenced by Max Talmey, a student who boarded with his family. Together they read and discussed texts by Leibniz and the *Critique of Pure Reason* of Immanuel Kant (1724–1804), another great German philosopher of the Enlightenment.

state of affairs, because obviously as soon as two observers disagree on the simultaneity of two events, they cannot agree about anything about time.

A new view of time

In particular, our two observers will never agree on duration—for instance, the time it takes a baby, traveling on the train, to drink a bottle. At the moment when the baby starts drinking, observer A activates his stopwatch; he stops

it at the moment when the baby finishes. Thus A considers two pairs of simultaneous events: first the starting of the needle of the stopwatch at zero, which for him is simultaneous with the first sucking motion by the baby, and then the moment when the needle stops, indicating, let us say, 6 minutes 10 seconds, which for him is simultaneous with the moment when the baby rejects the bottle. At this point he says: "This baby has drunk her bottle in 6 minutes and 10 seconds."

If observer B measures the time it takes the baby to drink the bottle, he will find, according to Einstein's calculations, a longer time. Einstein calls this the "dilation of time." Similarly, if B measures the width of the windows of the passing train, Einstein tells us that he will find a smaller width than the width measured by A, who is on the train, traveling with the windows. This is "length contraction." On the other hand, if B measures the height of the windows—that is, their dimension in a direction perpen-

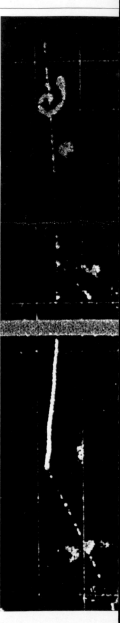

dicular to that of the motion of the train—he will find the same result as A; contraction of lengths only occurs in the direction of motion. Time dilation and length contraction are two main consequences of relativity theory.

Relativity, a matter of perspective

The relativistic effects of time dilation and contraction of lengths are comparable to the perceptual effect of optical perspective. As we have known since the Renaissance, par-

allel straight lines seen from a certain angle seem to meet; lengths that are known to be equal appear different; and the shape of objects may appear distorted. The theory elaborated in 1905 by Einstein shows us an effect of perspective that we had not expected: A and B see what is happening in the train from two different conceptual "angles"; this is translated into a shortening of lengths and a dilation of time.

These paradoxes concerning time and space have inspired a great deal of commentary and continue to excite the imagination. For many people, Einstein is the person who showed us that time is not absolute—not the same for everyone; and part of his prestige derives from the fact that he modified one of our most fundamental concepts of reality. From the beginning, the theory of relativity was understood to have serious philosophical implications. This was clearly evident when Einstein visited Paris in 1922 to lecture at the Sorbonne. World War I had ended not long before, and the political atmosphere was tense. The

The physicist George Gamow (1904–68), in his 1940 book *Mr. Tompkins in Wonderland,* introduced an office worker who, after reading a book on relativity, dreams that he is in a world where the speed of light is only 10 miles (16 km) per second, which makes it possible to observe certain effects foreseen by the theory: "The bicycle and the young man on it were unbelievably flattened in the direction of the motion...Mr. Tompkins felt very proud because he could understand what was happening to the cyclist—it was simply the contraction of moving bodies, about which he had just read." Far and near left: illustrations from Gamow's book.

One effect of the dilation of time is that the life span of a particle seems increased, when observed passing at a speed close to that of light. This dilation can be great enough to make particles observable, even those that exist for only a fraction of a millionth of a second before breaking down into other particles. Center: a photograph of such a subatomic particle, a muon, disintegrating in a cloud chamber, a device invented at the beginning of the 20th century by the physicist Charles Wilson (1869–1959) to detect particles in motion.

whole Parisian intelligentsia was on hand. Seated in the first row was the French philosopher Emile Bergson, author of *Duration and Simultaneity*, who did not fail to interrogate the great man. Legend has it that Einstein understood nothing of what Bergson was saying; it is not clear whether his knowledge of French was insufficient or whether deeper theoretical issues were responsible.

For physicists Einstein's importance was

You don't know a thing about the latest theories! Have you been living in a cave?

Your way of interpreti the relativity of space is shockingly naive!

not so much in the modifications he brought to our concepts of space and time, but rather the fact that he succeeded in liberating light from the concept of ether and subjected it to the same

principle as matter. From that time on, light was independent, propagating itself in the void, and there existed only one conceptual framework for examining the phenomena of matter and light: physics, which unified both.

September 1905: an important postscript

Four months after the publication of his article expounding the theory of relativity, Einstein added a three-page postscript, in which he demonstrated the most famous equation in all of physics: $E = Mc^2$, describing a relation-

Above, in blue and black: a letter from the Nobel committee to one of the nominators at the Collège de France concerning the award of the prize to Einstein.

And as for your grasp of the equilibrium of mass and energy—well, it's ridiculous!

J. Pruvost

Here, I'll give you my address; come see me and I'll explain it all to you.

Thank you. I'm afraid I haven't been in Paris very long…my name's Einstein.

ship between energy and mass. This was presented as an interesting consequence of the breakdown of the sharp division between matter and energy that his theory had brought about.

If a body emits a certain energy L in the form of light, Einstein demonstrated with the help of calculations that the mass of the emitting body has been diminished by a quantity equal to L/c^2, where c is the speed of light. He concluded that the mass of a body is linked to its energy content: if the body absorbs energy, its mass increases; if it loses energy, its mass diminishes. Mass (M) and energy (E) are thus equivalent; between the two there is only a simple conversion factor, which equals c^2. Therefore, $E = Mc^2$.

And Einstein added, as a precaution: "Perhaps it will prove possible to test this theory using bodies whose energy content is variable to a high degree (e.g., salts of radium)."

This forecast was confirmed in a spectacular way: nuclear energy—whether used for peaceful or military ends—results from the conversion of mass into energy as foreseen by the theory of relativity.

Einstein received the Nobel Prize in 1922 not for the theory of relativity—which some members of the prize committee considered too speculative—but for his work on photoelectric effect, which was considered to have useful industrial applications.

During World War I scientific exchanges had been broken off between Germany and other nations of Europe. In 1922, as part of the resumption of international academic relations, Einstein was invited to present his theories at the Collège de France in Paris. He caused a sensation and cartoonists in the popular press had a field day.

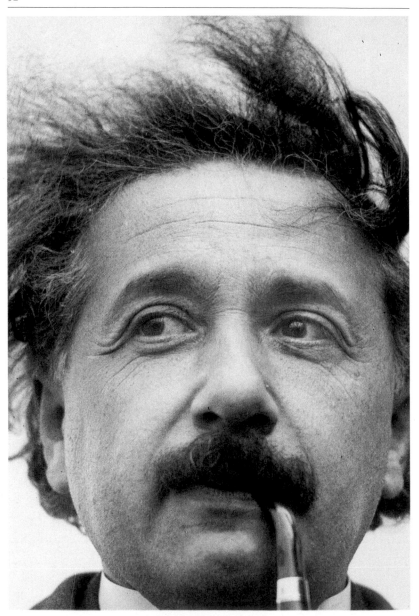

"I am now working exclusively on the gravitation problem…But one thing is certain: never before in my life have I troubled myself over anything so much…Compared with this problem, the original theory of relativity is child's play."

Albert Einstein,
letter to Arnold Sommerfeld, 1912,
translated by Anna Beck

CHAPTER 4
MATTER, SPACE, TIME

Left: Einstein in 1921; right: the actor Charlie Chaplin joins the Einsteins in 1931 for the premiere of his film *City Lights*.

Special relativity, general relativity

The theory of relativity as Einstein formulated it in 1905 failed to satisfy him. It is called the "special" theory of relativity because it explains how relativity works in special, controlled circumstances. Einstein therefore considered it incomplete. He thought that in a complete theory of relativity all objects in all circumstances ought to be equally subject to the laws of relativity.

Let us return for a moment to Galileo's principle of relativity, according to which the motion of a boat sailing at a constant speed in a straight line does not affect the behavior of a stone falling on the boat. The important word here is "constant": motion does not affect the behavior of the falling stone *only* when it is constant, at a uniform speed and in a straight line.

Why, Einstein wondered in 1907, should uniform motion have a privileged status? Wouldn't it be more satisfying to the mind if all points of view were equivalent, without any reference to motion? Put another way, shouldn't the principles of relativity function in any context? He added, joking, that anything else seemed an offense against the spirit of democracy. Thus he began to seek a "general" theory of relativity.

The law of falling bodies

There is little point in enunciating such a broad concept as a general theory of relativity unless it can provide the key to unexplained or puzzling phenomena. And indeed, general relativity allows us to understand why all bodies fall to earth at the same velocity.

Galileo had verified this phenomenon by experiment: he dropped several spheres with different masses, made of lead, stone,

Allgemeinen Relativitätstheorie

A bove left: Einstein's handwritten title, in German, for *Foundations of the General Theory of Relativity (Die Grundlage der allgemeinen Relativitätstheorie),* published in 1916.

B elow left: René Magritte's 1953 painting *Golconda* captures something surreal and mysterious about gravity: these men in bowler hats fall like raindrops, but seem to think they are immobile. Today, images of astronauts floating in space have made both the concept of gravity and the idea of zero gravity more familiar to us, yet Magritte's artwork has lost none of its provocative force. He has succeeded in illustrating the basic notion of relativity: that the points of view of different observers have equal validity.

wood, and paper, from the top of the Leaning Tower of Pisa, and they each took the same time to fall. Newton, working a generation later, had been unable to give a satisfactory explanation of this fact. He interpreted the falling of objects to the earth's surface as a particular example of a more general phenomenon: the attraction exerted between two bodies of matter—here, the earth and the object that falls—the concept known as gravity. Newton died without understanding the governing principle behind this idea. But his successors figured out that when objects are attracted by the pull of the earth's mass, that pull is the same for all objects, regardless of their mass. This pull is called the acceleration of gravity.

The general theory of relativity explains this riddle. Imagine two observers, X and Y. X is in free fall in an elevator that has a broken cable, while Y observes the

Newton was far from satisfied with his own explanation of gravity. On February 25, 1693, he wrote to the scholar Richard Bentley, "'Tis unconceivable that inanimate brute matter should (with the mediation of something else which is not material) operate upon & affect other matter without mutual contact, as it must if gravitation in the sense of Epicurus be essential & inherent in it. And this is one reason why I desired you would not ascribe innate gravity to me. That gravity should be innate, inherent & essential to matter so that one body may act upon another at a distance through a vacuum...is to me so great an absurdity that I believe no man who has in philosophical matters any competent faculty of thinking can ever fall into it. Gravity must be caused by an agent acting constantly according to certain laws, but whether this agent be material or immaterial is a question I have left to the consideration of my readers."
Left: a 1763 illustration lampooning his concept of the universal attraction of bodies.

Right: a 19th-century engraving illustrates Galileo's experiments in dropping spheres of different sizes and materials from the top of the Leaning Tower of Pisa.

event from the stairs nearby. X holds in her hand a stone, which she drops by opening her fingers, without giving it any speed.

She notes that the stone remains at her side, without moving. She is not surprised by this, since she explains the phenomenon by Newton's law of inertia, according to which "a body on which no action is taken always maintains the same speed" (null in this case, since X merely let the stone go, without giving it any acceleration).

According to the general theory of relativity, Y's point of view on the staircase must be equivalent to that of X in the elevator. Y explains what he sees (that the stone remains beside X) by saying that both are attracted by the earth and are pulled toward it, appearing to fall. To explain why the stone goes neither faster nor slower than X, he does not invoke Newton's law, but Galileo's, which states that "all bodies fall with the same movement, whatever their mass."

So the point of view of Y can be equivalent to that of X only if the law of falling bodies is true. In other words, the general theory of relativity is linked to the law of gravity, and mass and inertia are the same thing.

"If you knew all the trouble I had with mathematics!"

Einstein began to see the connection between the general theory of relativity and the mystery of gravity in 1907, but he did not formulate his complete theory until 1915. At the time it was said that only three people were capable of understanding its mathematical details. This is no doubt an exaggeration, but it is true that in order to develop his theory Einstein had to learn a great deal of new

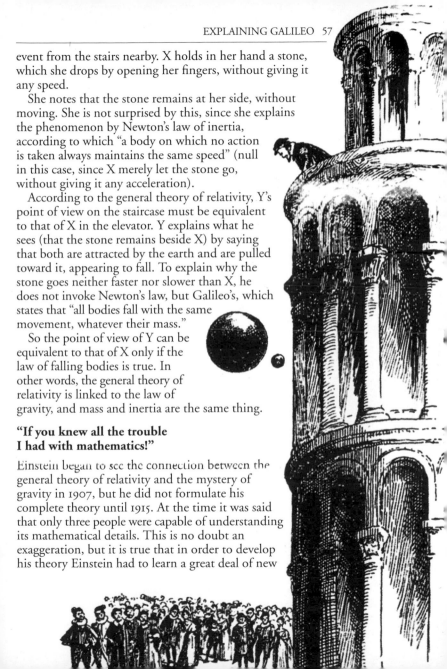

mathematics, of a sort that was too modern to have figured in his program of study the Polytechnic.

Meanwhile, in 1908 Einstein left the patent office. He obtained a university position, first in Bern and then, in 1911, at the German-language university in Prague. In 1912 he was appointed professor at the Polytechnic of Zurich—which represented a sort of sweet revenge for his initial rejection by the school as a young student. His old friend Marcel Grossmann was teaching mathematics there and Einstein requested his help in learning the mathematics necessary for the construction of his theory. Grossmann agreed, but stipulated that he would take no

Top: Einstein with his colleagues at the Zurich Polytechnic; above: the Kaiser Wilhelm Institute of Physics in Berlin in 1912.

responsibility for any physics concepts. The two men wrote several articles together; these always included a physics section signed by Einstein and a mathematics portion handled by Grossmann.

Still, the collaboration was not an entirely happy one. Their 1913 article, *Draft of a Generalized Theory of Relativity and of a Theory of Gravitation,* contained several errors in both the mathematics and the physics. It nevertheless caused a great stir in the scientific community. Soon Einstein was invited to teach in Berlin, the mecca of German science, and was elected to the prestigious Prussian Academy of

Thinking about relativity and the shape of space, Einstein "paid a visit in 1912 to my old school companion Marcel Grossmann [left], who in the meantime had become a mathematics professor at the Polytechnic. He became enthusiastic immediately, even though as a mathematician he would have been somewhat skeptical toward physics."

Although he detested Germany, Einstein had personal as well as professional reasons for leaving Zurich for Berlin in 1913. His marriage to Mileva

Sciences. Although he did not realize it at the time, this automatically made him a German citizen. He continued to work on the problem of gravitation and its connection to relativity. By November 1915, he had found his mistakes and revised his calculations. The result was a veritable avalanche of new results, which he presented at the Academy's weekly meetings. In the space of four successive Thursdays, the academicians were eyewitnesses to the birth of one of the most important theories of the century.

had collapsed, and though he did not blame her for it, his separation from her became "a matter of life or death," as he said later. In Berlin he met his cousin Elsa Einstein, whom he had known as a child in Munich and with whom he had been corresponding. They were to marry soon after the end of World War I, in June 1919.

Space is not what we thought

In order to establish the equivalence of all points of view, Einstein had to present mass and inertia as equivalent, which meant that the first problem to be solved was that of the nature of gravitation. Clearly, during the analysis of the falling stone in the falling elevator, X and Y attribute the motion of the stone to two different causes. In Y's view, gravity, the earth's attraction, causes the movement of the stone. From X's point of view, it is the absence of any force exerted on the stone that causes its motion—in this case, its immobility. For X, the space around the stone is in some way inert; whereas for Y, the space surrounding the stone seems to force it to move downward, that is, toward the earth.

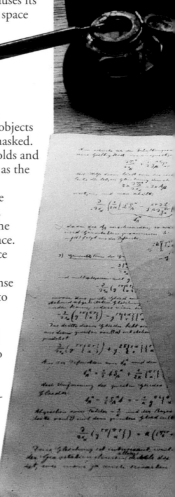

Who is correct? Both, of course, since their points of view are equivalent, according to the theory. Space always works on objects placed in it; however, this action is sometimes masked. In the case of X, for instance, the person who holds and then releases the stone is falling at the same rate as the stone, so that it looks motionless to her.

Inversely, objects also act on space. By its mere presence, the earth modifies the space around it, including the spot where the stone is located. The stone falls in response to the curved shape of space. Put simply: matter tells space how to curve; space tells matter how to move.

The two explanations are equivalent in the sense that they lead to the same result: the stone falls to earth with a uniformly accelerated motion. However, Einstein's conception allows us to understand why all bodies fall at the same speed to the surface of the earth: because they undergo the same deformation of space.

That space acts on objects placed in it and is modified by them is the most important innovation introduced by the general theory of relativity. Instinctively, we imagine space as an empty box in which objects are placed without changing the space inside the box. Classical physics—until 1915—did not change this intuitive conception of the world. Newton introduced forces between the objects

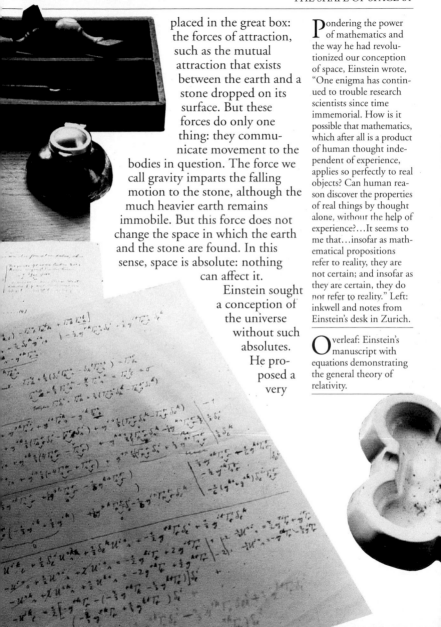

placed in the great box: the forces of attraction, such as the mutual attraction that exists between the earth and a stone dropped on its surface. But these forces do only one thing: they communicate movement to the bodies in question. The force we call gravity imparts the falling motion to the stone, although the much heavier earth remains immobile. But this force does not change the space in which the earth and the stone are found. In this sense, space is absolute: nothing can affect it.

Einstein sought a conception of the universe without such absolutes. He proposed a very

Pondering the power of mathematics and the way he had revolutionized our conception of space, Einstein wrote, "One enigma has continued to trouble research scientists since time immemorial. How is it possible that mathematics, which after all is a product of human thought independent of experience, applies so perfectly to real objects? Can human reason discover the properties of real things by thought alone, without the help of experience?…It seems to me that…insofar as mathematical propositions refer to reality, they are not certain; and insofar as they are certain, they do not refer to reality." Left: inkwell and notes from Einstein's desk in Zurich.

Overleaf: Einstein's manuscript with equations demonstrating the general theory of relativity.

Gravitation

$$g_{\sigma\tau}\, dx^2 + \cdots \cdots g_{\tau\tau}\, dt^2 = ds^2 \qquad\qquad \text{immer positiv für Punkt.}$$

$$\frac{ds}{dt} = H \text{ gesetzt.}$$

Bewegungsgleichungen

$$\frac{d}{dt}\left(\frac{\partial H}{\partial \dot{x}}\right) \rightarrow \frac{\partial H}{\partial x} = 0 \qquad\qquad \frac{d}{dt}\left(\frac{\partial \varphi}{\partial \dot{x}}\right) = -\frac{\partial \varphi}{\partial x}$$

$$\frac{\partial H}{\partial \dot{x}} = \frac{g_{11}\dot{x} + g_{12}\dot{y} + \cdots + g_{44}}{\frac{ds}{dt}}$$

$$\sqrt{g}\; g_{11}\dot{x} + g_{12}\dot{y} + \cdots = \cdots \cdot \; \varrho\sqrt{g}\left(g_{11}\frac{dx}{ds}\frac{dt}{ds} + g_{12}\frac{dy}{ds}\frac{dt}{ds} + \cdots\right)$$

der Bewegungsgrösse pro Volumeneinheit

Tensor der Bewegung von Massen $\quad T_{ik}^{b} = \varrho_0 \frac{dx_i}{ds}\frac{dx_k}{ds}$

Tensor der Bewegungsgrösse, Energie $\quad \left\{ T_{m\sigma} = \sqrt{g}\sum g_{m\nu} T_{\nu\sigma}^{b} \right|$

Negative

(Ponderomotorische Kraft pro Volumeneinheit $\quad \frac{1}{2}\sqrt{g}\sum_{\mu\nu}\frac{\partial g_{\mu\nu}}{\partial x_{m}} T_{\mu\nu}^{b}$

$$\sum_{\nu m}\frac{\partial}{\partial x_\nu}\left(\sqrt{g}\, g_{m\nu} T_{\nu m}\right) - \frac{1}{2}\sqrt{g}\sum_{\mu\nu}\sqrt{g}\,\frac{\partial g_{\mu\nu}}{\partial x_m} T_{\mu\nu} = 0$$

Setzen wir $\sqrt{g}\, T_{\sigma\nu} = \Theta_{\sigma\nu}$

$$\sum_{\mu\nu}\frac{\partial}{\partial x_\mu}\left(g_{m\mu}\,\Theta_{\mu\nu}\right) - \frac{1}{2}\sum_{\mu\nu}\frac{\partial g_{\mu\nu}}{\partial x_m}\Theta_{\mu\nu} = 0 \qquad \text{Im Allgemeinen ungeordneten Pkt.}$$

Gilt für jeden Tensor z. B. $\sqrt{g}\, \gamma_{\mu\nu}$

$$\sum_{\mu\nu}\frac{\partial}{\partial x_\mu}\left(\sqrt{g}\, g_{m\mu}\gamma_{\mu\nu}\right) - \frac{1}{2}\sum_{\mu\nu}\left(\sqrt{g}\,\frac{\partial g_{\mu\nu}}{\partial x_m}\gamma_{\mu\nu}\right) = 0 \text{ oder Vierervektor}$$

$$\underbrace{\qquad\qquad}_{\dfrac{\partial\sqrt{g}}{\partial x_m}} \qquad\qquad \frac{1}{\sqrt{g}}\frac{\partial\sqrt{g}}{\partial x_m}$$

Stimmt:

Nochmalige Berechnung des Elementtensors

$$\frac{1}{2}\left(\frac{\partial^2 g_{im}}{\partial x_k \partial x_l} + \frac{\partial^2 g_{kl}}{\partial x_i \partial x_m} - \frac{\partial^2 g_{il}}{\partial x_k \partial x_m} - \frac{\partial^2 g_{km}}{\partial x_i \partial x_l}\right)$$

$$-\frac{1}{4}g_{\varrho\sigma}\left(\frac{\partial g_{i\varrho}}{\partial x_l} + \frac{\partial g_{l\varrho}}{\partial x_i} - \frac{\partial g_{il}}{\partial x_\varrho}\right)\left(\frac{\partial g_{k\sigma}}{\partial x_m} + \frac{\partial g_{m\sigma}}{\partial x_k} - \frac{\partial g_{mk}}{\partial x_\sigma}\right)\bigg|\, g_{kl}$$

$\frac{1}{2}g_{kl}\frac{\partial^2 g_{im}}{\partial x_k \partial x_l}$ bleibt stehen.

$$g_{kl}\left[\begin{smallmatrix}kl\\i\end{smallmatrix}\right] = g_{kl}\left(2\frac{\partial g_{il}}{\partial x_k} - \frac{\partial g_{kl}}{\partial x_i}\right) = \sigma \;\bigg|\; \frac{\partial}{\partial x_m}$$

$$g_{kl}\left[\begin{smallmatrix}kl\\m\end{smallmatrix}\right] \quad g_{kl}\left(2\frac{\partial g_{mk}}{\partial x_l} \doteq \frac{\partial g_{kl}}{\partial x_m}\right) = \sigma \;\bigg|\; \frac{\partial}{\partial x_i}$$

$$g_{kl}\left(\frac{\partial^2 g_{il}}{\partial x_k \partial x_m} + \frac{\partial^2 g_{mk}}{\partial x_i \partial x_l} - \frac{\partial^2 g_{kl}}{\partial x_i \partial x_m}\right) + \frac{\partial g_{kl}}{\partial x_m}\left(2\frac{\partial g_{il}}{\partial x_k} - \frac{\partial g_{kl}}{\partial x_i}\right) + \frac{\partial g_{kl}}{\partial x_i}\left(2\frac{\partial g_{m}}{\partial x_l} - \frac{\partial}{\partial x_l}\right)$$

$$\frac{1}{2}g_{kl}\left(\quad\right) = \frac{1}{4}\left|\frac{\partial g_{kl}}{\partial x_m}\left(2\frac{\partial g_{il}}{\partial x_k} - \frac{\partial g_{kl}}{\partial x_i}\right) + \frac{\partial g_{kl}}{\partial x_i}\left(2\frac{\partial g_{mk}}{\partial x_l} - \frac{\partial g_{kl}}{\partial x_l}\right)\right.$$

zweites Glied:

$$-\frac{1}{4}g_{\varrho\sigma}\frac{\partial g_{l\varrho}}{\partial x_i}\frac{\partial g_{k\sigma}}{\partial x_m}g_{kl} \quad\longrightarrow\quad +\frac{1}{4}\frac{\partial g_{k\sigma}}{\partial x_i}\frac{\partial g_{k\sigma}}{\partial x_m}\; gl\,g_{k}$$
$$\;-\frac{1}{4}\frac{\partial g_{k\sigma}}{\partial x_l}\frac{\partial g_{k\sigma}}{\partial x_m}$$

$$-\frac{1}{4}g_{\varrho\sigma}\left(\frac{\partial g_{i\varrho}}{\partial x_l} - \frac{\partial g_{il}}{\partial x_\varrho}\right)\left(\frac{\partial g_{m\sigma}}{\partial x_k} - \frac{\partial g_{mk}}{\partial x_\sigma}\right)g_{kl}$$

$$-\frac{1}{2}g_{\varrho\sigma}g_{kl}\frac{\partial g_{i\varrho}}{\partial x_l}\frac{\partial g_{m\sigma}}{\partial x_k} + \frac{1}{2}g_{\varrho\sigma}g_{kl}\frac{\partial g_{il}}{\partial x_\varrho}\frac{\partial g_{m\sigma}}{\partial x_k}$$

Den mit 2 multiplizierte Elementtensor erhält also die Form

$$g_{kl}\frac{\partial^2 g_{im}}{\partial x_k \partial x_l} - \frac{1}{2}\frac{\partial g_{kl}}{\partial x_m}\frac{\partial g_{kl}}{\partial x_i} + \frac{\partial g_{kl}}{\partial x_m}\frac{\partial g_{il}}{\partial x_k} + \frac{\partial g_{kl}}{\partial x_i}\frac{\partial g_{mk}}{\partial x_l}$$

$$-g_{\varrho\sigma}g_{kl}\frac{\partial g_{i\varrho}}{\partial x_l}\frac{\partial g_{m\sigma}}{\partial x_k} + g_{\varrho\sigma}g_{kl}\frac{\partial g_{il}}{\partial x_\varrho}\frac{\partial g_{m\sigma}}{\partial x_k}$$

Resultat sicher. Gilt für Koordinaten, die der Gl. $\Delta\varphi = 0$ genügen.

different vision of the world, in which the objects placed in space—the earth, the stone, the sun, you, me—modify it and are also affected by the modifications produced by the other bodies.

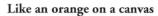

Like an orange on a canvas

Just what is this modification? It is by no means easy to grasp. Only complex mathematics can provide a true description. Let us use simpler models. Imagine that space is like a canvas stretched on a frame. If nothing is placed on the canvas, it is flat; but if we put an orange on it—representing the earth, for instance—this object would make a small dent on the surface of the canvas and would deform the area surrounding it.

Now let us put a marble on the edge of the canvas and release it—this marble represents the stone that is dropped. It rolls along the line of greatest incline until it reaches the orange (the earth). Newton said that the

When we speak of Einstein's concept of space as modified or distorted by the bodies within it, it is common to describe space as "curved."

If it is curved, then the shortest distance between two points is not a straight line, as Euclidian geometry states, but a curve, and Euclidian geometry does not describe the reality of the world.

Below: a fanciful depiction of curved space.

marble (the stone) is attracted by the orange (the earth); but it is equally possible to state, with Einstein and all physicists since, that the orange (the earth) has modified space—it has deformed space by inscribing a dent—and that the marble (or stone), without anyone having

The curve produced in space by the presence of a mass can be represented if we imagine an orange placed on a stretched canvas; the

touched it, rolls naturally along the line of greatest incline. The advantage of this concept is that it allows us to see immediately that all the marbles—whether made of lead, wood, or paper— necessarily follow the same trajectory, which is entirely determined by the orange; in other words, all bodies that "fall" to earth do so in the same motion—as Galileo had stated.

orange creates an indentation. A heavier object, such as a planet, produces a greater indentation.

Time and space do not exist without matter

In the general theory of relativity, space is not only modified by the bodies found in it, but cannot exist without these bodies. Simply stated: it is matter that creates space. It is impossible to empty space of all matter, because then space too would disappear.

To make matters more confusing, when we speak of space, we should really call it space-time, because the world is not three-dimensional, as we imagine it to be, but four-dimensional. It has height, width, and depth, the three dimensions of space, and a dimension of time. (Even the earlier special theory of relativity had mixed space and time together.)

Thus not only space but also time disappears if the world is emptied of matter. Difficult though it is to comprehend, matter creates at once both space and time.

"Seven A.M. Arrived in New York. Worse than the most fantastic expectation. Hordes of reporters came on board…plus an army of photographers who pounced on me like hungry wolves. [They] asked exquisitely stupid questions, to which I replied with cheap jokes, which were enthusiastically received."

Albert Einstein's travel diary,
December 11, 1930,
translated by Ewald Osers

CHAPTER 5
THE USES OF FAME

Left: Einstein in 1930. In 1922 Einstein took a trip to Paris organized by Walther Rathenau, the foreign minister of the German Republic and a champion of French-German reconciliation. While there, he received this card [right]: "You are beautiful, you are great, and you come from the land of work and morality. Mighty genius devoted to the good of humanity, accept this expression of deepest admiration from a French worker. [Signed] C. Demay, Paris, 3/6/22."

Vous êtes beau, vous êtes grand, et vous êtes des pays du travail et de la moral.
Puissant génie au service bienfaisant de l'humanité. Recevez toute l'admiration d'un ouvrier français.
C. Demay
Paris. 6/3/22

Einstein refutes Newton

As early as 1911 Einstein was urging astronomers to test relativity theory by measuring the movement of light to see if gravity deflected its trajectory. He had questioned the traditional concept that light rays pass through space in a straight line, and predicted that observations would prove that they were affected by the modification of space (or more precisely, of space-time) that results from the masses found in it. Light ought, he said, to follow a curved path. He had calculated the deflection of the light rays emanating from a certain star, located behind the sun, as they passed close to the sun while moving toward earth; from his measurements of the star's light he had

"Newton forgive me...
The concepts that you created still dominate the way we think in physics, although we now know that they must be replaced by others."
Albert Einstein,
Autobiographical Notes,
1946, quoted in
Banesh Hoffmann,
Albert Einstein:
Creator and Rebel, 1972

Left: Einstein visiting New York, c. 1920.

"The description of me and my circumstances in *The Times* shows an amusing feat of imagination on the part of the writer. By an application of the theory of relativity to the taste of readers, today in Germany I am called a German man of science, and in England I am represented as a Swiss Jew. If I come to be regarded as a *bête noire,* the descriptions will be reversed, and I shall become a Swiss Jew for the Germans and German man of science for the English."
Albert Einstein, letter to
The Times (London),
November 28, 1919

deduced that the star ought to appear at a different location from the expected one.

But one can only see a star located behind the sun when the sun is in total eclipse and its blinding light diminished; thus, the deflection of light that Einstein predicted can only rarely be observed, during total solar eclipses.

In August 1914 a team of German astronomers had been commissioned to make observations during a total solar eclipse visible in Siberia. But World War I broke out a few days before the date of the eclipse; the astronomers were taken prisoner by the Russians and Einstein's prediction remained unconfirmed. Five years later, a solar eclipse on May 29, 1919, offered a new opportunity for some British astronomers to look for the deflection of stellar light as it passed the sun. An expedition led by Sir Arthur Stanley Eddington (1882–1944) to the equatorial island of Principe, observed and photographed the passage of stellar light. On his return to England, the photos were analyzed: the star was indeed just where

T op: Einstein on the cover of a German magazine in December 1919. Above: on September 22 of that year a Dutch colleague, Hendrik Lorentz (1853–1928), sent a telegram to Einstein: "Eddington found star deflection around rim of sun. Preliminary measurements between nine-tenths second and double." Einstein's fame did not thrill everyone in Germany: starting in 1920 he became the target of an organized antisemitic campaign. Outside of Germany, his German nationality was held against him.

L eft: crowds greet Einstein in New York.

Einstein had said it would be. On being so informed by telegram, he is reputed to have replied: "I knew all the time that the theory was correct. [Otherwise] I'd have to feel sorry for God."

Thus, on November 6 of that year, four years after Einstein's completion of the general theory of relativity, Eddington announced to a joint meeting of the Royal Society and the Royal Astronomical Society in London that he had confirmed Einstein's theory and negated that of Newton. The portrait of Newton, an early president of the Royal Society, gazed down on the historic moment.

The event immediately unleashed an unprecedented media storm. Teletypists all over the world spread the news, and newspapers published editorials on it in the morning editions. In one night, Einstein, who had been an obscure university professor, became a living legend.

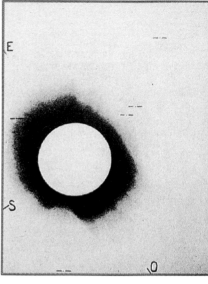

A brilliant celebrity

Why was this arcane scientific event so celebrated? We must remember that World War I had just ended and Europe was emerging from more than four years of fratricidal slaughter. The fact that British astronomers had verified a German theory was immediately perceived and presented by a number of pacifist, internationally minded journalists as a symbol of peace regained. It was proof that science was capable of transcending nationalisms and could be a factor for peace making. Today such visions seem idealistic and perhaps illusory, but in 1919 the world had not yet

"When I was in England I got the impression that the scientists there are less prejudiced and more objective than our German scientists. But I must point out that quite a number of well-known English scientists were pacifists and refused war duties; i.e., [Arthur] Eddington and [Bertrand] Russell."

Albert Einstein, letter to Arnold Sommerfeld, July 13, 1921

Left: Eddington in 1921. He was a scientist, a Quaker, a conscientious objector, an unconditional champion of the general theory of relativity, and an advocate of friendship among nations. Above: the May 1919 solar eclipse, photographed in Brazil.

Left: a page from the *Illustrated London News,* November 22, 1919, depicting the curvature of light rays as confirmed by photographs taken during the recent solar eclipse.

"All England has been talking about your theory," Eddington wrote to Einstein in December 1919, with barely disguised pride. Eddington's persistence was greatly responsible for making Einstein famous. It cannot have been a simple matter, so soon after the war, to raise the funds for two expeditions halfway around the world for the purpose of proving the rather obscure theory of a German scientist, merely because it might constitute "one of the finest examples of the effectiveness of mathematical reasoning." But none of these obstacles mattered to Eddington. He was also optimistic enough not to despair when rain—which had been predicted at Principe Island for three weeks—started to fall just as the eclipse was beginning.

become aware of the destructive potential represented by science's mastery of nature. Eddington wrote to Einstein, "It is the best possible thing that could have happened for scientific relations between England and Germany."

The pacifist creed

Einstein himself did not fully share this optimism; in any case, he did not mince words concerning the international nature of science. He wrote in 1922, "The greatest effect of the sciences is not of an intellectual but rather a material nature. Technical discoveries have largely internationalized economic processes. This has led to the transformation of any future war into a matter of international importance." And he added: "When this factual status has entered human consciousness, people will have sufficient goodwill to prevent wars." This declaration sums up rather well the kind of political role he hoped to play: that of a man of peace.

Einstein had not waited for the war to end before demonstrating his pacifist convictions. In 1914, Germany was swept with nationalist fervor and war fever. Nearly the whole Berlin intelligentsia signed a petition backing the German army and its leaders as guardians of German culture, and going so far as to denounce "the shameful spectacle of Mongols and Negroes being driven against

War broke out in August 1914; in October he coauthored an "Appeal to Europeans," a manifesto addressed to all responsible people. "The struggle raging today can scarcely yield a 'victor,' he declared. "All nations that participate in it will, in all likelihood, pay an exceedingly high price."

the white race." Einstein refused to sign, but rather joined another Berlin colleague in issuing an "Appeal to Europeans," calling on intellectuals to use all their influence to stem the eruption of nationalist passions. Aside from its authors, only two persons signed this appeal.

Einstein's political efforts during the war had little effect, however, both because it was such an unfavorable period for pacifists and because he was absorbed by his work on the general theory of relativity. As a Swiss citizen, he was not subject to the German draft. His complicated personal life was also a distraction. He and Mileva separated in 1914, and in 1919 he married his cousin Elsa, with whom he had been conducting an affair for some time; moreover, exhausted by his work, he had been almost continuously ill during 1917 and 1918.

But the end of the war and his newfound fame seemed to offer him an ideal opportunity to demonstrate his political convictions. He decided that despite his reluc-

"The importance of securing international peace was recognized by the really great men of former generations. But the technical advances of our times have turned this ethical postulate into a matter of life and death for civilized mankind today, and made the taking of an active part in the solution of the problem of peace a moral duty which no conscientious man can shirk."

Albert Einstein, *The World as I See It*, 1934, translated by Alan Harris

tance it was his duty not to turn his back on his sudden celebrity but rather to use it to advance the causes near to his heart—above all, the cause of peace. If the mythic figure of Einstein was largely a media creation, it can justly be said that he contributed to it considerably for reasons of personal ethics.

Between 1919 and 1933 (when he had to flee Germany) Einstein was prominently active on several pacifist fronts, primarily through the Commission for Intellectual Cooperation of the League of Nations. In this context, he worked to oppose a boycott against German science organized by the victorious Allied Powers. At the same time, he led a committee to inves-

"The benefits that the inventive genius of man has conferred on us in the last hundred years could make life happy and carefree if organization had been able to keep pace with technical progress. As it is, these hard-won achievements in the hands of our generation are like a razor in the hands of a child of three."

Albert Einstein on a planned 1932 disarmament conference, *The World as I See It*, 1934, translated by Alan Harris

Below: Einstein speaking in Berlin, 1930.

tigate war crimes committed by the German army in Belgium, but he resigned from the commission in 1923 to protest the French army's occupation of the Ruhr district of Germany, part of a punitive war-reparations program imposed by the Allies. And throughout the 1920s he voiced strong support for conscientious objectors, who at the time were subject to prose-cution, writing letters on their behalf to judges and politicians. "Following the disappointing results of the disarmament conferences," he wrote in 1931, "I came to the conviction that the world can be progressively delivered from the scourge of war only by persons who have had the courage to sacrifice themselves by refusing all military service."

Adolf Hitler's accession to power in 1933 forced him to change his mind on the subject.

His own definition of Judaism

Along with the defense of peace, the cause of the Jewish people was one of the most frequent issues of Einstein's activism. He had been born into a family that was Jewish by race but atheist by inclination, and that, like many German Jews, strove for assimilation into mainstream society. It was apparently during his stay in Prague in 1911–12 that he developed a more detailed idea of what it meant to be Jewish.

EINSTEIN   FREUD   STEINACH

Copyright, 1931, by
The New York Times Company.

THE ROAD T

The Noted Scientist, With the D
Material Disarmament, and C

"When I read 'of German citizens of the Jewish faith,'" he wrote in 1920, "I cannot avoid a wry smile. What is concealed behind that pretty name? What is Jewish *faith*? Is there a kind of non-faith through which one ceases to be a Jew? No." And he added, "To speak of faith is a way of hiding that what characterizes a Jew is not his faith but his membership in the Jewish nationality. We must learn again to take pride in our history, and as a people

NOVEMBER 22, 1931.   TWENTY-FOUR PAGES

EACE—BY EINSTEIN

nt Conference in View, Calls for Mental as Well as
lan to Help Free the World From War's Menace

we must resume the cultural tasks that can renew our community feeling."

This is the essence of Einstein's understanding of Judaism. He reacted hopefully, therefore, to the Balfour Declaration of November 2, 1917, in which Britain pledged to create a Jewish national home in Palestine, which was under British control at the end of World War I. He campaigned for the creation of a high-level university in Palestine—"not a farmers' college"—and in 1921 agreed, at

Above, far left: a 1931 caricature of Einstein and Sigmund Freud, together with the Austrian biologist Eugen Steinach, is hardly flattering. In 1932 Einstein and Freud conducted a correspondence, which the League of Nations published as a pamphlet entitled *Why War?* They were frequently named as among the world's most eminent Jews.

Near left: Albert Einstein and the French physicist Paul Langevin (1872–1946) during a 1923 antimilitarist demonstration in Berlin. The two shared strong pacifist convictions and a common vision of theoretical physics. Below: a headline from the *New York Times Magazine* of November 22, 1931.

Below, far left: Einstein and the chemist and physicist Marie Curie during a meeting in Geneva in 1922, when the two worked together on the Commission for Intellectual Cooperation of the League of Nations. They had known one another for many years and maintained both a professional and familial friendship, spending a summer vacation together with their children, hiking in the Swiss Alps in July 1913.

the request of Chaim Weizmann (1874–1952), leader of the World Zionist Organization, to tour the United States to raise funds for it. "Naturally," he noted bluntly, "I am needed not for my abilities but solely for my name, from whose publicity value a substantial effect is expected among the rich tribal companions in Dollaria."

Until the end of his life Einstein maintained a strong interest in the development of the Hebrew University in Jerusalem, spending a great deal of time and diplomacy to settle its internal conflicts and helping to establish programs in mathematics and physics there.

In the wake of the Balfour Declaration, Jewish settlers poured into Palestine, hoping to fulfill their long-held dream of founding a Jewish state. Einstein admired their hard work and accomplishments, but he could not overlook the fact that they were moving into lands some of which belonged to Arabs. He commented on the subject several times, unequivocally condemning both Jewish and Palestinian extremists, particularly during the Arab uprisings in Jerusalem in 1929.

He placed more confidence than was reasonable in the power of his expressed opinions, hoping—too optimistically—that the British government would ensure harmonious relations between the two communities. In the 1930s his conviction that a Jewish homeland was desirable was reinforced by the rise of virulent antisemitism in Germany and the assault on Jews during World War II. He thus accepted the creation of the state of Israel in 1948 as a necessity imposed by circumstances.

After World War I, Palestine came under control of the British government, which honored the 1917 Balfour Declaration. Below: Lord Balfour at the inauguration of the Hebrew University in Jerusalem, 1925.

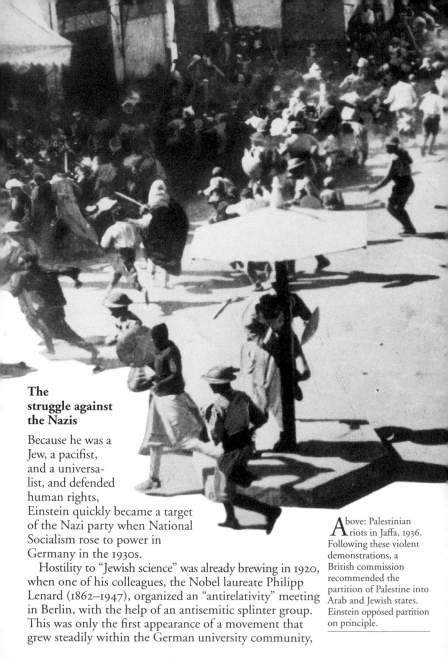

The struggle against the Nazis

Because he was a Jew, a pacifist, and a universalist, and defended human rights, Einstein quickly became a target of the Nazi party when National Socialism rose to power in Germany in the 1930s.

Hostility to "Jewish science" was already brewing in 1920, when one of his colleagues, the Nobel laureate Philipp Lenard (1862–1947), organized an "antirelativity" meeting in Berlin, with the help of an antisemitic splinter group. This was only the first appearance of a movement that grew steadily within the German university community,

Above: Palestinian riots in Jaffa, 1936. Following these violent demonstrations, a British commission recommended the partition of Palestine into Arab and Jewish states. Einstein opposed partition on principle.

counting Lenard as one of its leaders. Known as "German science," the movement aimed to purify science of "non-Aryan" traces. Relativity theory and quantum theory were its favorite targets. After Hitler gained control of the government in 1933, Jewish scientists were promptly driven from the universities; soon it was forbidden even to pronounce the name Einstein.

Einstein left Germany in 1933. That is, he was traveling in the United States when, in late January, Hitler took power. On his return to Europe he decided not to go back to Berlin, but went instead to Belgium. He sent a letter of resignation to the Prussian Academy of Sciences, not wishing to depend on a government that "denies equality of rights before the law as well as freedom of speech and expression."

The Russian chemist and Zionist Chaim Weizmann, with whom Einstein traveled to the United States in 1921, became the first president of the state of Israel in 1949.

As the situation in Germany deteriorated, he accepted an invitation from the recently established Institute for Advanced Study at Princeton University in New Jersey, which opened its doors to a number of prestigious refugees during the 1930s.

Thus Einstein emigrated to the United States in 1933. In Princeton he set up a comfortable home with his wife, Elsa, until her death in 1936. His elder stepdaughter, Ilse, died in Paris in 1934, but the younger, Margot, soon also came to live in Princeton with her husband. As war loomed, Einstein's sister, Maja, and his elder son, Hans Albert, also came to America. His schizophrenic younger

son, Eduard, remained in Zurich, cared for by Mileva. In 1934 the German government formally canceled Einstein's citizenship. He became a U.S. citizen in 1940. During this time he participated actively in the rescue of German Jews, especially numerous academics who had fled to France, England, or the United States, and who were offered no splendid positions like his. He refused all contact with the professors who remained in Germany and even developed, late in life, a downright primitive hatred of Germans, something rather astonishing in a man usually grounded in rationalism.

Familienname (be

Bornamen (Rufnar

Familienstand:

Bor- und Familien-(C
des (bzw. früheren)

On March 28, 1933, Einstein resigned from the Prussian Academy, writing: "Throughout 19 years the Academy provided me with the opportunity to devote myself to scientific work… However, dependence on the Prussian government, entailed by my position, is something that, under the present circumstances, I feel to be intolerable." Left: a 1933 caricature of Einstein; right: Nazis and German students burning "non-German" books in Berlin, May 10, 1933; above and below: details of the German document canceling Einstein's German citizenship in 1934.

Vorstehend bezeichn
am | durch

Der Deutscher
Bekanntmachun
Deutschen Re
1934.

Ort und Datum:

Geburtsname): **E i n s t e i n**

rstreichen): **Albert**

lebig	verheiratet	verwitwet	geschieden

ame

: *Elsa geb. Einstein*

ist rechtskräftig verurteilt worden:

wegen	auf Grund von	zu	Bemerkunge

tsangehörigkeit für verlustig erklärt durch
24.3.1934, veröffentlicht in der Nr.75 des
zeiger u. Preußischen Staatsanzeigers vom 29.3

Unterschrift (Behörde):

Weekend getaway

Einstein loved to sail, whether before the war at his lakeside chalet at Caputh, near Potsdam, or after, in the United States, off Long Island, New York.

From his mother Einstein inherited a lifelong love of music. As to his actual skill on the violin, opinions varied. In any case, chamber music played an important part in his life. He even played some concerts in Carnegie Hall as a benefit for one of the innumerable humanitarian causes he supported. During sea voyages, on the great steamers that took him to Japan, the United States, or Latin America, he enjoyed playing trios and quartets with other passengers. Left: playing the violin in 1931; above right: on shipboard the same year; below right: during a chamber-music concert.

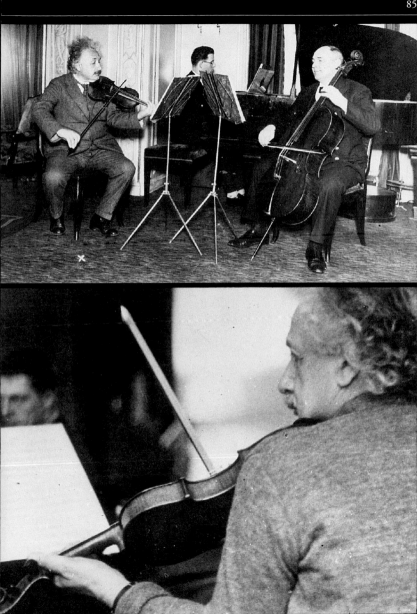

Exile in Princeton

Einstein lived for 22 years in the United States, mainly in Princeton, a golden retreat where he had no obligations but to mix with intellectuals as famous as himself. Throughout these decades he was constantly asked for his opinion on all subjects, and never evaded inquiries.

Concerning his political life in the United States, much attention has been paid to a letter he sent to President Franklin D. Roosevelt on August 2, 1939 (exactly one month before World War II began) urging him to start a program to construct a nuclear bomb, lest the Germans succeed first. This letter indicates that Einstein's pacifist philosophy had its limits. What happened next is now well known: in 1941 American and émigré physicists and technicians formed the Manhattan Project. They gathered at Los Alamos, a sort of military camp deep in the desert of New Mexico, and built a nuclear bomb, detonating tests in July 1945. The following month two atomic bombs were dropped on the Japanese cities of Hiroshima and Nagasaki, killing hundreds of thousands of

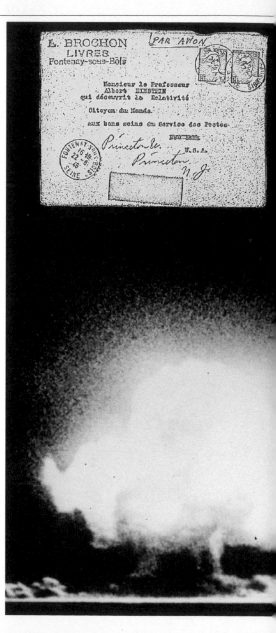

civilians, destroying the cities, and putting an end to the war with Japan.

Einstein did not work on the Manhattan Project, and the science used to develop nuclear weapons did not derive directly from his research. But his formula $E = Mc^2$ described the enormous amount of energy locked into even a small amount of ordinary matter. Other scientists discovered how to release this energy in the form of nuclear explosions. Throughout the war, however, he made it clear that he supported the national effort to develop nuclear energy and bombs.

Afterward, from 1945 until his death in 1955, he resumed his efforts on behalf of peace. He lent his moral authority to the Emergency Committee of Atomic Scientists, an organization created by some of the participants in the Manhattan Project who were disturbed by the state's and the army's grip on scientific research. He also joined actively in the resistance by many American intellectuals to the anticommunist political hysteria that reigned during the 1950s, in the era of McCarthyism. He intervened especially in the case of Ethel and Julius Rosenberg, a married couple, communists and physicists, who had been convicted of treason on ambiguous evidence and were executed. His final political act, and also his last piece of writing, was a republication of his 1914 "Appeal to Europeans," a plea to scientists to abolish war, written with the English philosopher Bertrand Russell.

With the growing arsenals of the superpowers, Einstein feared global destruction. "The only salvation for civilization," he told a reporter in 1945, "…lies in the creation of world government, with security of nations founded upon law…As long as sovereign states continue to have separate armaments and armaments secrets, new world wars will be inevitable."

"Einstein is demanding that the atom bomb should not be handed over to other countries, especially Russia…The 'world government' demanded by [him] seems to have been created in the image of Standard Oil, with managers and managed—[he has] a brilliant brain in his own subject, housed in a bad violinist and eternal schoolboy with a penchant for generalizing about politics."

Bertolt Brecht,
Journal, October 28, 1945

Left: the first test of an atomic bomb, near Los Alamos, New Mexico, July 16, 1945; inset: a 1946 postcard from an admirer, mailed from France, is addressed simply to "Mr. Einstein who discovered Relativity, Citizen of the World, postal service: please deliver, USA." Someone has kindly added, "Princeton U., Princeton, N.J."

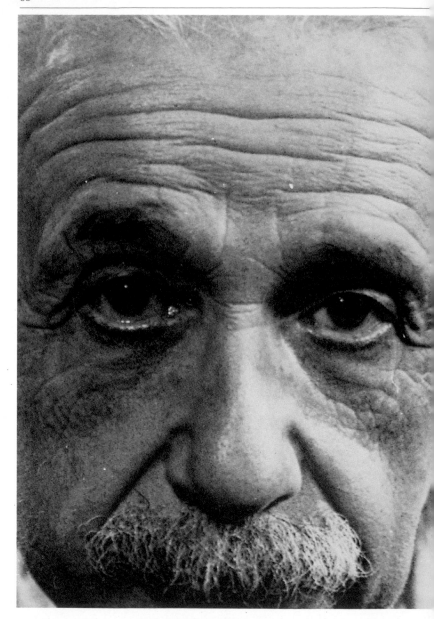

"The discussions with Einstein have extended over many years…which have witnessed great progress in the field of atomic physics. Whether our actual meetings have been of short or long duration, they have always left a deep and lasting impression on my mind, and when writing this report I have, so to say, been arguing with Einstein all the time."

Niels Bohr,
"Discussion with Einstein on
Epistemological Problems in Atomic Physics," 1949, in
Albert Einstein: Philosopher-Scientist, pp. 240–41

CHAPTER 6
THE OLD MAN ALONE

"[Bohr] utters his opinions like one perpetually groping and never like one who believes he is in possession of the definite truth."
Albert Einstein,
letter to B. Becker,
March 20, 1954

Left: Einstein in 1947; right: Niels Bohr in 1925, at the time of the publication of the first papers on quantum theory.

"I once again sang my old solitary song"

Thus Einstein expressed himself in 1949 in a letter to the Danish physicist Niels Bohr (1885–1962). This was how he was ending his life as a physicist: like an aged relative to whom one listens out of courtesy and respect for his years and his glorious past, patiently waiting for him to finish his speech, but attaching little meaning to it.

Einstein's views diverged substantially from those of the physicists of the following generation, primarily over the question of the status of quantum theory. He had helped to create this branch of theoretical physics by establishing the concept of light quanta, but to the end of his life he disliked many of its subsequent ideas.

Quantum physics was concerned with the nature and behavior of atoms and subatomic particles. In developing a theory to describe these, it rejected the intuitions of classical physics, including the basic notion that if data are known about the present location and momentum of a particle, its future momentum and location may be predicted. Thus, it was named "quantum mechanics," to distinguish it from the laws of Newtonian mechanics. Quantum mechanics largely abandoned the traditional description of elementary physical objects—electrons, protons, even in some cases whole atoms—as localized objects that move on well-defined trajectories. The concrete language of classical physics was ill-equipped to describe the structure of an atom—for example, an attempt to picture an electron as the negatively charged particle that circles around the nucleus of an atom was quickly

In his later, less productive years, Einstein accepted a great many invitations to lecture, and traveled frequently. In 1932 he visited California and found congenial company among American astronomers, who were interested in the cosmological consequences of general relativity. With them he found a sort of shelter from the "quantum virus" that was invading European universities. Left: lecturing at the Carnegie Institute of Technology in Pittsburgh in 1934; below: a poster announcing a lecture by Einstein in Berlin in February 1927: "Theoretical and Experimental Considerations of the Question of the Propagation of Light."

Mathem.-physikalische Arbeitsgemeinschaft an der Universität Berlin

Mittwoch, 23. Februar 1927, abends 8¼ Uhr

Universität, Auditorium Maximum (122)

VORTRAG

Prof. Dr. A. Einstein

„Theoretisches und Experimentelles zur Frage der Lichtentstehung"

abandoned. Quantum mechanics was able to express the fact that, in certain circumstances—for instance in an electron microscope—an electron can follow an infinite number of trajectories at the same time.

By the rules of Newtonian physics this notion makes no sense. In this and other ways, quantum theory introduced the element of uncertainty into physics, running counter to the most basic principle of classical science, which insists that states and behaviors of elements are measurable and predictable according to fixed laws.

The Solvay Congress of 1927

The controversy between Einstein and the younger scientists arose in the 1920s,

when they began to construct quantum theory on the basis of ideas he had proposed in 1905. Just as the concept of relativity had rethought such basic Newtonian premises as the sharp distinction between matter and energy, so now quantum theory explained the behavior of atoms in ways that Einstein's relativity theory could not. The group included Werner Heisenberg (1901–76) and Pascual Jordan (1902–80) from Germany, the Viennese Wolfgang Pauli (1900–58), and Niels Bohr, who was their leader, as well as the older German physicist Max Born (1882–1970). They would have loved to enjoy the approval of the man they considered their spiritual father. Einstein, for his part, would have liked to be able to applaud the exploits of these young physicists, for whom he felt much admiration and affection. Bohr,

Ed. HERZEN Th. DE DONDER E. SCHROEDINGER   W. PAULI W. HEISENBERG   L. BRILLOUIN

R. H. FOWLER

E. VERSCHAFFELT

H. A. KRAMERS   P. A. M. DIRAC   A. H. COMPTON   L. V. de BROGLIE   M. BORN   N. BOHR

H. A. LORENTZ   Å. EINSTEIN   P. LANGEVIN   Ch. E. GUYE   C. T. R. WILSON

Absents : Sir W. H. BRAGG, MM. H. DEBLANDRES et E. VAN AUBEL

O. W. RICHARDSON

In the interwar period, the Solvay Congresses were select scientific conferences with a limited number of hand-picked participants. They were often imitated, never equaled. Near left: the 1927 Solvay Congress, attended by luminaries of 20th-century physics, including 13 past and future Nobel laureates, among them Erwin Schrödinger (1887–1961), Bohr, Heisenberg, and Louis de Broglie (1892–1987). Einstein is seated front row, center.

To amuse his colleagues, in 1932 the biologist Max Delbrück (1906–81) wrote and presented a satire on Goethe's *Faust*. The physicist George Gamow drew the illustrations for the program. Opposite: Niels Bohr, Paul Ehrenfest, Wolfgang Pauli, and Einstein caricatured as figures from the tale; below: the program cover; far left: Max Planck (at far left) with Einstein and some government ministers in Berlin in 1931.

in particular, had charmed him with the depth of his thinking: "Meeting and knowing you has been one of the strongest experiences of my life," Einstein wrote to him—a rare effusion from one who tended to spare the superlatives. The rift that developed in their views of science was thus painful for both sides.

Einstein rejected the concepts of quantum theory in the harshest terms. When he read the first quantum papers in 1925, he remarked famously, "Heisenberg has laid a big quantum egg." The quantum physicists were focusing their research on the nature and behavior of the atom, a subject that Einstein considered secondary.

The theoretical differences between Einstein and his young admirers, especially between Einstein and Bohr, took a spectacular public turn in 1927, during the fifth Solvay Congress. Ernest Solvay was a Belgian industrialist who had made his fortune by inventing a process for manufacturing sodium and financed high-caliber scientific congresses that met in Brussels.

The 1927 Solvay Congress was the forum chosen by the Young Turks of

FAUST
EINE HISTORIE

MANUSKRIPT: J. W. v. Goethe
REGIE: Stoakregende des Institut für teoretisk Fysik.

MOTTO:
Nicht um zu kritisieren
H. Hohn.

atomic physics to exhibit the results of their research. They expected resistance from Einstein, but they also hoped to convince him. But Einstein raised persistent objections that forced them to buttress their reasoning. According to legend, the arguments against the new theory that Einstein presented at dinner were refuted the next morning at breakfast by Bohr, who had spent the night thinking.

Ehrenfest between Einstein and Bohr

Paul Ehrenfest (1880–1933), an Austrian physicist working in Holland, played an important role in this theoretical confrontation. He had been a friend of Einstein since 1911. Although of the same generation as Einstein, he was open to Bohr's arguments and often acted as an intermediary between Einstein and his young colleagues.

The younger physicists found Einstein's hostility hard to understand. They saw themselves in the same position toward him as he had been in 1905, when he faced the adversaries of his new theories. Bohr wrote of this period: "I remember, also, how at

Despite sharp differences of opinion, Bohr and Einstein maintained an enduring friendship that clearly meant a great deal to both of them. This did not prevent them from waging a fierce and famous intellectual combat. Left and right: Bohr and Einstein photographed by Ehrenfest in 1927, during the Solvay Congress.

Below: Paul Ehrenfest was close to Bohr and Einstein and a gifted physicist in his own right. He contributed significantly to the elaboration of quantum theory and figured centrally in the controversy that divided his two friends.

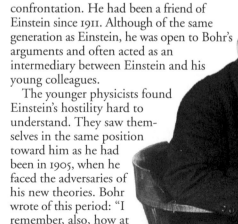

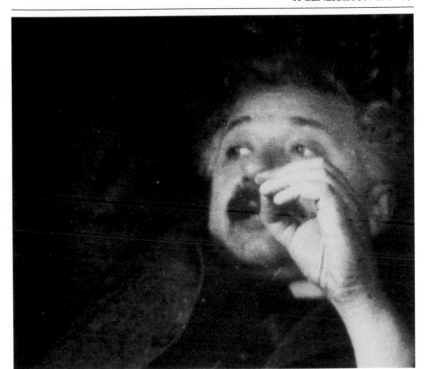

the peak of the discussion Ehrenfest...jokingly hinted at the apparent similarity between Einstein's attitude and that of the opponents of relativity theory; but instantly Ehrenfest added that he would not be able to find relief in his own mind before concord with Einstein was reached."

Einstein's objections, which he repeated for twenty years, focused on an aspect of quantum theory called probability. According to probability theory, an element of an atom—an electron, for instance—can take an infinite number of paths at the same time. This means that if its position is measured at a given instant it is impossible to obtain a single result, as would have been the case if the electron were a marble—or a planet. Thus, the theory predicts that an electron's position can be defined only as a probability: all that can be said is that the electron has a certain probability of having a certain location at a certain instant.

"It was, of course, a lie what you read about my religious convictions... I do not believe in a personal God and I have never denied this but have expressed it clearly. If something is in me which can be called religious then it is the unbounded admiration for the structure of the world so far as our science can reveal it."

Albert Einstein, quoted in Helen Dukas and Banesh Hoffmann, eds., *Albert Einstein: The Human Side*, 1979

Einstein could not accept the idea that the position of an electron could not be predicted with certainty. He would not be satisfied with probabilities. "God," he remarked, "does not roll the dice."

The quest for unity

All efforts to reconcile quantum theory with Einstein's views proved fruitless. He continued to believe that it would remain incomplete and approximate, though he recognized some of its brilliant successes. While other physicists embraced quantum mechanics with increasing enthusiasm, he maintained his solitary opinion to the end.

In part he was distracted by another direction of inquiry, which occupied him for the rest of his life. Having completed the special and general theories of relativity, he began to look for a grand overarching theory—called the unified field theory—that would describe in a single system of equations the properties of light, matter, and gravitation (or, more precisely: the unity of gravity and electromagnetism, and two other forces, called the strong and weak nuclear forces). He thought that it ought to be constructed on the model of the two theories of relativity—that is, by beginning with certain basic principles. The explanation of electron behavior, which he felt was so inadequately described by quantum theory, would necessarily derive from these principles. He even hoped to deduce the existence of subatomic particles from an extension of general relativity theory.

For two decades Einstein worked on the unified field theory. He never succeeded in constructing it. "You imagine that I look back on my life's work with calm satisfaction," he wrote in a letter to Maurice Solovine in 1949. "But from nearby it looks quite different. There isn't a single concept of which I am convinced that it will stand up, and I feel unsure if I am even on the right road. My contemporaries, however, see me as a heretic and a reactionary who has, as it were, outlived himself."

"Dear Schrödinger: You are the only contemporary physicist, besides [Max von] Laue, who sees that one cannot get around the assumption of reality—if only one is honest. Most of them simply do not see what sort of risky game they are playing with reality—reality as something independent of what is experimentally established. They somehow believe that the quantum theory provides a description of reality, and even a *complete* description."

Albert Einstein,
letter to Erwin
Schrödinger,
December 22, 1950

Below: the physicist's office at the Institute for Advanced Study, Princeton, 1955; right: Einstein in Princeton, 1938.

"Today scientists describe the universe in terms of two basic partial theories—the general theory of relativity and quantum mechanics. They are the great intellectual achievements of the first half of this century…Unfortunately, however, these two theories are known to be inconsistent with each other—they cannot both be correct. One of the major endeavors in physics today…is the search for a new theory that will incorporate them both—a quantum theory of gravity."

Stephen Hawking,
A Brief History of Time, 1988, pp. 11–12

CHAPTER 7
EINSTEIN'S LEGACY

Einstein proposed the existence of gravitational waves as a consequence of his general theory of relativity. Left: the scientist late in life; right: the constellation of Virgo, in whose galaxies the emission of gravitational waves has been detected.

Throughout his life Einstein was a man alone. In Bern, at age 25, after finishing his workday at the patent office, he sat alone each evening rebuilding physics on a new foundation. In Berlin he struggled without respite to work out the general theory of relativity, so much more resistant than expected. At Princeton he worked like Homer's Penelope, undoing each previous day's work in order to start afresh, and trying in vain to transform the general theory of relativity into a unified field theory embracing all of nature's forces. Meanwhile, all around him, younger people busied themselves developing quantum mechanics, the fruits of his imaginative mind.

Einstein, in other words, never belonged to a working team. In this respect he truly lived in another age, for most scientific research today is unthinkable without organized, well-staffed laboratories supported financially within academia, government, or industry. Even in his own time, he was something of a dinosaur, since the collective work model that rules research today was developed between the two world wars. The first great laboratories were founded in Germany, England, France, and the United States just at the time when Einstein was becoming a world-famous scientist.

He offers a striking contrast to the other great physicist of his era, Niels Bohr. Before he had turned 30, Bohr strove to create a scientific community. As a professor at the University of Copenhagen in 1921 he obtained funding to

Berlin in Einstein's day was a great center of both experimental science and modern art, and the two spheres were not always unrelated. Below: the Einstein Tower of the Astrophysics Laboratory at Potsdam, outside Berlin. The architect was Erich Mendelsohn (1887–1953), whose innovative Expressionist style was strongly influenced by the breakthroughs in physics early in the century. The tower is considered one of his masterworks; Einstein, however, did not like it.

establish an Institute of Theoretical Physics, which he opened up to young researchers from all over the world. In this fertile hothouse, students and teachers stayed up far into the night in passionate discussion. Einstein, on the other hand, had no true heirs, though he attracted acolytes. At most, at certain points in his life he developed close collaborations with mathematicians, starting with Marcel Grossmann. At Princeton he had a whole choir of young co-workers, who found themselves less students than assistants.

The Einstein Tower, completed in 1922 after Einstein won the Nobel Prize, was paid for by the German government and a foundation. It was equipped with instruments intended to prove several of his astronomical predictions, including the gravitational red shift, which was, however, not confirmed until the 1960 Harvard experiment of Pound and Rebka. Left: Einstein on a balcony of the tower; below: one of Mendelsohn's preparatory sketches for the building.

Einstein's legacy in quantum mechanics

Einstein is also the last of the classical physicists in the sense that he never truly accepted quantum theory and its dependence upon the concept of probability. He maintained to the end of his life that quantum mechanics, far from being the full-fledged theory that its promoters imagined, was incomplete. He argued that "hidden variables" existed, which, if eventually discovered, would reestablish the classical model of the measurability and predictability of the laws of the universe. "Some day," he wrote to Tatyana Ehrenfest, the widow of Paul Ehrenfest, "a theory will emerge that will avoid the statistical nature [of this work] and will force the theory to include a greater number of magnitudes."

Nonlocality

At Princeton in 1935 he wrote a famous short article critiquing quantum mechanics, in collaboration with two other physicists, Boris Podolsky and Nathan Rosen. The paper presented the so-called EPR paradox—the initials of the three authors—which argued that quantum theory was capable of describing only certain aspects of the physical universe. The argument went like this: according to quantum theory, two particles, A and B, that have interacted at a point in their history but have long since ceased to interact (and may be far separated in space), continue to affect one another. This is the principle of nonseparability, usually called nonlocality. Atomic particles are causally related to one another even at a distance. Einstein noticed what seems to be a logical problem with this idea: if one measures particle A without measuring particle B the result will be different than if one had also measured B. This contradicts basic common sense.

Below left: Einstein walking in the garden in his last years.

The paper drew two possible conclusions: either quantum mechanics is incomplete and must be completed in such a way as to restore common sense; or else it is true, in which case it must be admitted that two objects that have interacted are never totally separate, even if they are countless millions of miles away from one another. Obviously, Einstein preferred the first solution.

He was mistaken. It has since been demonstrated—both theoretically and experimentally—that quantum mechanics is neither wrong nor incomplete. But he had hit upon an essential trait of quantum physics: two objects that have interacted are never totally separate; the fact that this shocks us and runs counter to our strongest intuitions is irrelevant.

It is probable that if Einstein had not raised the specter of nonlocality, it would have taken some time to make itself felt. Nonlocality is one of the most surprising characteristics of quantum theory: it places the very nature of material things in doubt. We are accustomed, in the physical world, to think of objects as discrete from one another, and we have trouble imagining that a different system might hold true at the microcosmic level. Einstein's legacy in the field of quantum physics is thus largely made up of open questions and problems raised, which he has forced his successors to confront, obliging them to explore more deeply the "absurd" nature of the quantum world.

In *Mr. Tompkins in Wonderland* Mr. Tompkins and his companions are attacked by what appears to be a group of tigers in the quantum jungle. A friend aims between the eyes of the closest tiger and misses. " 'Shoot more!' shouted the professor. 'Scatter your fire all round and don't mind about precise aiming! There is only one tiger, but it is spread around our elephant.' " Like an electron that is not usually found at one precise location, the tiger is everywhere at once. The property of nonlocality, or quantum entanglement, is even more surprising: particles that have once interacted are linked; a change in the behavior of one causes an instantaneous change in the behavior of the other, even when they are separated by great distances. In 1964 an Irish physicist named John Bell made the first calculations to disprove the EPR paradox. In 1982 a team led by the French physicist Alain Aspect went further, conducting experiments with pairs of photons (light particles) in which a change in the orbit of one produced a simultaneous change in the orbit of the other, with no time gap at all, regardless of how far separated the two were. Nonetheless, the debate between Einstein's position and the idea of nonlocality has not yet been resolved.

"A theory that only three persons are capable of understanding"

Einstein's all-time favorite invention was the general theory of relativity, which had cost him so much effort, and which he tried for 30 years to generalize even further. Yet celebrated though it was, the theory of relativity was dealt with by only a very small number of physicists. Public opinion was that its calculations were so difficult that only three physicists in the world understood it. Legend has it that on hearing this claim, Eddington (who had conducted the expedition that verified part of the theory) responded: "I'm just wondering who the third one might be."

For a long time the general theory of relativity remained a magnificent theoretical object whose implications were too abstract to be useful and whose effects, situated at the cosmic level, seemed unlikely ever to be observed.

For a long time the theory of relativity was considered incomprehensible except to its author and a few experts. Today it is taught in introductory physics courses. What has changed is the way it is perceived by physicists. In the 1950s general relativity was considered to relate to mathematics rather than to physics, which concerned itself with practical problems: building radio receivers, producing nuclear energy, and so on. Einstein himself was often referred to as a mathematician.

1959–60: year of rebirth

All this changed abruptly between September 1959 and September 1960, when several experiments confirmed some attributes of the universe predicted by relativity theory. First, on September 14, 1959, the planet Venus reached the point in its orbit closest to the earth. For the first time, researchers at the Massachusetts Institute of Technology were able to send a radar signal in its direction and to detect the echo of the signal as it returned to earth. Measurement of the time it takes a radar signal to reach a celestial object and return allows an extremely precise determination of its distance from the earth. Thus, this experiment marked the start of a new era, in which the entire solar system became accessible to high-precision measurement.

The rapid development in the 1960s of programs of satellite exploration accelerated this area of research.

Above: a 1950 cartoon illustrates the perplexity with which Einstein's ideas were often met.

Today, distances within the solar system are known with sufficient precision to allow us to measure the infinitesimal deflections of space-time foreseen by general relativity.

New observations, new theories

The next decisive event was the measurement in 1960 by two American researchers, Robert Pound and Glen Rebka, of another infinitesimal effect foreseen by Einstein's theory. The theory asserted that the wavelength of light changes as it falls, within a gravitational field (such as that of the earth). This is called the "gravitational red shift," since the light, in falling, appears redder—though not to the naked eye, and only to an observer who is not traveling with the light source. The measurement was carried out between the top and bottom of a building at Harvard University, only 74 feet (22.5 meters) high, so the effect was very small; it was only possible because ultrasensitive detectors of light wavelength had become available.

Marvelous instrumentation was created during the 1950s and 1960s; and then inventions in technology boomed with the construction of ever more precise lasers and semiconductors. Most of these inventions grew out of quantum theory, which also developed rapidly in these decades.

Measurement of the gravitational red shift was carried out by Pound (above) and Rebka (below) at Harvard University. The experimenters, one sitting at the head of an elevator shaft at the top of the Jefferson Building, the other at the bottom, in the basement, carried out the experiment by telephone.

A third event affecting relativity theory took place during the summer of 1960. A young English mathematician named Roger Penrose (born 1931) published new calculation techniques for application to the study of general relativity that proved much more effective and simpler than the older computational technology, which had been extremely dense and cumbersome. Penrose won widespread recognition, and today everyone knows the name of one of the theoreticians who used his new method: Stephen Hawking (born 1942). He and other young physicists soon began to report exciting new discoveries.

At the end of the same summer, two American researchers, Carl Brans (born 1935) and Robert H. Dicke (1916–1997), proposed a theory intended to replace general relativity (published in 1961). Although the new, competing theory ultimately did not prove superior to the former one, its announcement had a strong impact on relativity physicists, who were obliged to issue more precise data and definitions in the face of its challenge.

Finally, 1960 was the year in which new objects began to be discovered in the heavens, and could not be explained without reference to general relativity. One summer night, astronomers using the great Mount Palomar telescope in California discovered something that looked like a new star where they were expecting to observe a diffuse brightness. Since this object showed a very quickly variable luminosity and emitted primarily radio waves, it was baptized a "quasi-stellar radio source," quasar for short. Quasars are not stars, though they may look similar to observers on earth; currently they are thought to be gigantic black holes absorbing stars and radiating massive amounts of energy.

The relativists wake up

The large red shifts detectable in the light emitted by quasars tell us that they are moving away from us at a fantastic speed, so that we ought not to see them as brilliant objects. These mysterious objects puzzled and awakened relativity physicists, who had been in a

The renaissance of general relativity in 1960 also marks the birth of a new discipline: relativistic astrophysics, which held its first congress in Dallas in December 1963. The scientists who gathered there to discuss the origins of quasars did not yet call themselves astrophysicists but mathematicians, astronomers, or physicists. It was an occasion filled with comical misunderstandings, since they had as yet no common terminology with which to discuss the new discoveries. Above: a quasar.

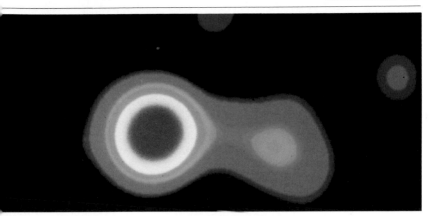

theoretical doze, and they began to imagine various possible explanations for their origin. In the ensuing years, as telescopes and other observational and measuring devices improved, other strange celestial objects and phenomena turned up. These included black holes, which seem to be stars that have collapsed, creating areas in space whose gravitational field is so great that not even light particles can escape from them; and the even more mysterious pulsars, also thought to be collapsed stars, which emit radio or other waves at regular intervals, usually of about one second. (Some have a faster signal, and some also emit energy at other wavelengths, producing a blinking light.) Today, general relativity

Roger Penrose in the 1960s. Penrose is primarily a mathematician, but he excelled in the field of relativity, particularly in the study of black holes, along with his compatriot, Stephen Hawking. Among other things, he developed the Penrose diagram, which creates a visual representation of the effect of gravity upon an object as it moves near a black hole.

embraces an immense field of observation and investigation.

This second birth of general relativity is largely due to the availability of new equipment and new theoretical tools. Most useful of all are today's powerful computers, which can analyze immensely complex data taken from observed images. As the study of general relativity continues to widen, the basic theory— once understood by "only three persons"—has become a standard subject for students in college and even high school.

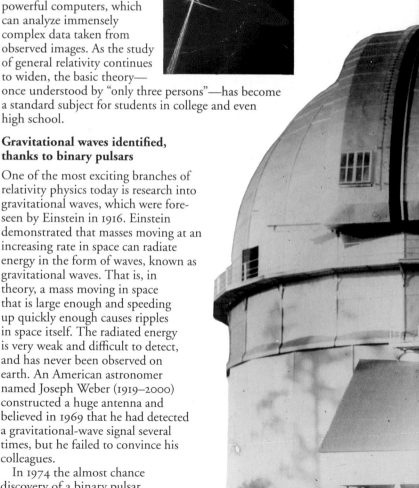

Left: a painting of a pulsar. Below: Einstein visiting Mount Wilson Observatory in California in 1931.

Gravitational waves identified, thanks to binary pulsars

One of the most exciting branches of relativity physics today is research into gravitational waves, which were foreseen by Einstein in 1916. Einstein demonstrated that masses moving at an increasing rate in space can radiate energy in the form of waves, known as gravitational waves. That is, in theory, a mass moving in space that is large enough and speeding up quickly enough causes ripples in space itself. The radiated energy is very weak and difficult to detect, and has never been observed on earth. An American astronomer named Joseph Weber (1919–2000) constructed a huge antenna and believed in 1969 that he had detected a gravitational-wave signal several times, but he failed to convince his colleagues.

In 1974 the almost chance discovery of a binary pulsar

revolutionized the detection of gravitational waves. A binary pulsar is a pair of stars—whence the adjective "binary"—one rotating around the other, that emit light at precisely regular intervals (whence the name "pulsar"). The revolving motion of the one star must, according to Einstein's theory, emit gravitational waves. The close presence of pulsar emissions of light provided an accurate means of measuring these gravitational emissions. Starting in 1974, scientists began observing this binary pulsar, searching for evidence of wave emissions in the behavior of the revolving star. No one expected quick results, but in 1979, during a colloquium held to mark the centenary of Einstein's birth, a team of American researchers announced that they had found a minute alteration in the speed of each star's revolution around its partner, indicating a loss of energy due to the emission of gravitational

A pulsar is a star at the end of its life. It emits radio waves in a beam that sweeps around as the star rotates, like a lighthouse beam. Each time it sweeps past a wave detector on earth a "pulse" is registered. The first binary pulsar, called PSR 1913+16, was discovered in 1974 and led to the first, indirect proof of the existence of gravitational waves. It has an orbital period of only eight hours, so measurements of it are very precise. Scientists calculated how much the speed of its orbit should be reduced by a loss of energy due to the emission of gravitational waves. They then measured tiny actual reductions in the speed of its orbit and found that these matched predictions to within 0.5 percent.

Below: a telescope at the Royal Observatory at Greenwich, England, emits a laser beam.

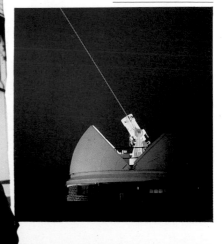

waves, as predicted by Einstein's calculations. Since then, the search for gravitational waves, like many other areas of inquiry inspired by relativity theory, has led to vast research projects such as LIGO, the Laser Interferometer Gravitational-Wave Observatory, now being constructed in the United States.

The quest for black holes

Black holes are another type of object foreseen by Einstein's theory. Like the concept of space-time, they are a popular subject in science fiction. Let us recall that a mass deforms the space-time surrounding it, as an orange would do if placed on a stretched canvas. Black holes have an extremely strong concentration of matter: one with the mass of our sun would have a diameter of just 2 miles (3.2 kilometers). The curvature of space-time caused by this enormous concentration of matter is so strong that every object approaching it is immediately pulled into it, never to be released. Light particles are no exception: they cannot escape from the hole, which for this

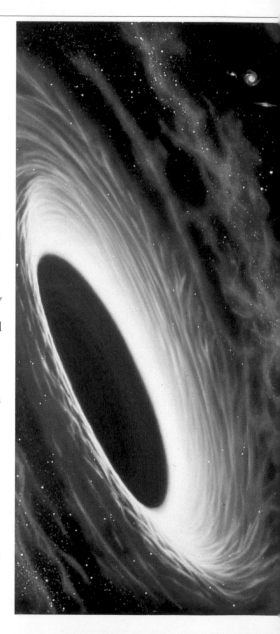

reason is termed "black." These objects therefore cannot be observed, but their existence has been inferred—for example, by the presence of dust orbiting around a compact and massive, but invisible, object in space; and by the presence of quasars. It is not possible to prove that such observed data can only be explained by the presence of a black hole, rather than some other phenomenon, but the idea is now generally accepted.

Black holes have contributed enormously to the renewal of interest in general relativity theory, and the hunt for them has led to numerous other theoretical projects.

The impossible union of quantum theory and general relativity

Einstein fathered two theories: quantum theory, which he rejected once the child grew up; and general relativity, which always remained his favorite. Physicists today must try to reconcile the two. They understand the structure of space-time very differently. Whereas the space-time of quantum theory is passive, a sort of theater in which particles act, the space-time of general relativity is produced by particles and cannot exist without them. This conceptual difference makes the two theories incompatible.

Physicists are at an awkward impasse, for both theories remain valid despite repeated attempts to disprove them. General relativity has been resisting such attempts for nearly a century, while quantum mechanics has led to so many applications in modern technology that it is difficult to imagine it could be wrong. History seems to be repeating itself, since physicists today find themselves in nearly the same situation as their predecessors in 1905: facing the need to reconcile two apparently incompatible theories. Physics awaits a new Einstein who, inspired by a simple, radical insight, will resolve this contradiction.

Two types of stellar systems are currently serious contenders for the title of black holes: certain X sources—that is, emissions in the area of X-rays—called jumpers (there are five possible candidates at the moment) and quasars, whose enormous energy emissions seem connected to the presence of a black hole. The observational status of black holes is still poorly defined, and it is too soon to select definitely any of the candidates that have appeared. Left: an artist's rendition of a black hole; above: a *Washington Post* cartoon.

Overleaf: when President Truman announced plans to develop a hydrogen bomb in 1950, Einstein spoke out vehemently against the idea on national television.

DOCUMENTS

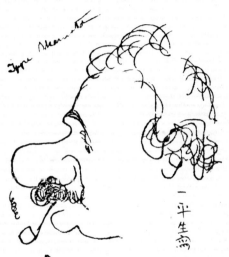

Early love

History has not been very kind to Mileva Marić, the woman Einstein married in his youth and later divorced with such evident relief. Yet Marić was herself a talented scientist, able to understand the groundbreaking ideas Einstein was exploring at the turn of the century.

P revious page: caricature of Einstein by Ippei Okamoto; above: Einstein and Mileva.

Marić to Einstein, Heidelberg, after October 20, 1897:

It's been quite a while since I received your letter, and I would have answered immediately to thank you for your sacrifice in writing a four-page letter, thus repaying a bit of the enjoyment you gave me during our hike together—but you said I shouldn't write until I was bored—and I am very obedient (just ask Fräulein Bächtold). I waited and waited for boredom to set in, but until today my waiting has been in vain, and I'm not sure what to do about it. On the one hand, I could wait until the end of time, but then you would think me a barbarian—on the other, I still can't write you with a clear conscience…

I don't think the structure of the human skull is to be blamed for man's inability to understand the concept of infinity. He would certainly be able to understand it if, when young, and while developing his sense of perception, he were allowed to venture out into the universe rather than being cooped up on earth or, worse yet, confined within four walls in a provincial backwater. If someone can conceive of infinite happiness, he should be able to comprehend the infinity of space— I should think it much easier. And human beings are so clever and have accomplished so much, as I have observed once again here in the case of the Heidelberg professors…

It's such an old story how much human beings think they know. You could sit and listen to them for the rest of your life and they would still be regaling you with all that they have discovered. It really was too enjoyable in Prof. Lenard's lecture yesterday; now he's talking about the kinetic theory of gases. It seems that oxygen molecules travel at a speed of over 400m per second, and after calculating and calculating, the good professor set up equations, differentiated, integrated, substituted, and finally showed that the molecules in question actually do move at such a velocity, but that they only travel the distance of 1/100 of a hair's breadth...

Einstein to Marić, Zurich, Wednesday, February 16, 1898:
Dear Fräulein,
...I'm glad that you intend to return here to continue your studies. Come back soon; I'm sure you won't regret your decision. I am convinced that you will be able to catch up rather quickly on our most important course work. Still, it's most embarrassing for me to have to recount the material we've covered. Only here will you find the material properly organized and explained.

Hurwitz lectured on differential equations, except for partials, as well as Fourier series, and some on the calculus of variations and double integrals. Herzog spoke very clearly and well on the strength of materials, and somewhat superficially on dynamics, but that's to be expected in a "mass course." Weber lectured masterfully on heat (temperature, heat quantities, thermal motion, dynamic theory of gases). I eagerly anticipate every class of his. Fiedler is lecturing on projective geometry; he's the same indelicate rough person he always was, and a little impenetrable at that, though he's always brilliant and profound. In short: a master but unfortunately a terrible pedant too. The only other important course that will give you much to do is number theory, but you

Einstein's friend, the chemist and physicist Marie Curie. She won the Nobel Prize twice, in 1903 and 1911; Einstein won in 1922.

can make it up gradually by studying on your own...

But now back to the books. Best wishes, your

Albert Einstein

Einstein to Marić, Milan, Monday, March 13 or 20, 1899:
...Your photograph had quite an effect on my old lady. While she studied it carefully, I said with the deepest sympathy: "Yes, yes, she certainly is a clever one." I've already had to endure much teasing about this, among other things, but I don't find it at all unpleasant.

My musings on radiation are beginning to take on more substance—I myself am curious if anything will come of it.

Best wishes *etc.*, especially the latter, from your

Albert
My old lady sends her best.

Einstein posing for a photographer, c. 1920.

Einstein to Marić, early August, 1899:
D[ear] D[ollie],

You must really be surprised to see my hieroglyphics again so soon, especially since you know how lazy I am when it comes to writing letters.

Here in Paradise I live a nice, quiet, philistine life with my mother hen and sister—it's just as the pious and the upright imagine paradise to be. In my spare time I've studied quite a bit of Helmholtz on atmospheric movements—but out of my fear of you (as well as for my own pleasure), I hasten to add that I promise to reread it with you later. I admire the originality and independence of Helmholtz's thought more and more. You, poor girl, must now stuff your head with gray theory, but I know that with your divine composure, you'll accomplish everything with a level head. Besides, you are at home being pampered, as a deserving daughter should

be. But in Zurich you are the mistress of our house, which isn't such a bad thing, especially since it's such a nice household! When I read Helmholtz for the first time I could not—and still cannot—believe that I was doing so without you sitting next to me. I enjoy working together very much, and find it soothing and less boring.

My mother and sister seem somewhat petty and philistine to me, despite the sympathy I feel for them. It is interesting how gradually our life changes us in the very subtleties of our soul, so that even the closest of family ties dwindle into habitual friendship. Deep inside we no longer understand one another, and are incapable of actively empathizing with the other, or knowing what emotions move the other…

Einstein to Marić, Thursday, August 10?, 1899:
D[ear] D[ollie],

…The vacation offers me peace and quiet, so it is the studying that is a welcome diversion for me, not the loafing—just the opposite of the situation in our household. And you, good soul, write me that cramming agrees with you—that's what I like to hear. You're such a robust girl and have so much vitality in your little body. I returned the Helmholtz volume and am now rereading Hertz's propagation of electric force with great care because I didn't understand Helmholtz's treatise on the principle of least action in electrodynamics. I'm convinced more and more that the electrodynamics of moving bodies as it is presented today doesn't correspond to reality, and that it will be possible to present it in a simpler way. The introduction of the term "ether" into theories of electricity has led to the conception of a medium whose motion can be described, without, I believe, being able to ascribe physical meaning to it. I think that electrical forces can be directly defined only for empty space, something also emphasized by Hertz. Further, electrical currents will have to be thought of not as "the disappearance of electrical polarization over time," but as the motion of true electrical masses whose physical reality appears to be confirmed by electrochemical equivalents. Mathematically they can then always be understood in the form $\frac{\partial x}{\partial x}$ +.+. Electrodynamics would then be the theory of the movements of moving electricities and magnetisms in empty space: which of the two views prevails depends on the results of the radiation experiments.— By the way, I haven't heard anything from Rector Wüest yet. I'll write to him soon.

Here in Paradise it is always very beautiful, especially since we have such wonderful weather. We are always having unpleasant visits from Mother's acquaintances though…

Einstein to Marić, Milan, Tuesday, October 10, 1899:

D[ear] S[weet] D[ollie],

Now that's a fine way to behave! You've already been comfortably taking your exams for four days now and I, your good colleague and fellow coffee-guzzler, have yet to hear so much as a peep out of you. Isn't that shocking? I'll have to rehearse a stern sermon for when I see you next Monday—it will be held as early as possible. And if the girl at the door says that you've gone out and I see your shiny little boots in front of the door—as sometimes happens—then I'll just wait a bit more or go get a shave.

I'm taking my sister to Aarau on Sunday and will arrive at my dear ex-landlady's house in Zurich the very same day. She simply hasn't answered the postcard in which I dared to ask if it was within her "infinite capacity for foresight" to find me lodgings somewhere else. In other words, I, the poor little parcel, must wait for delivery until someone finds me an address. When I think how you must now be buried in work, my anger about your not writing me melts away like wax. You poor thing, you've really had it a lot harder than I had it in the last year, being so alone and all. But wait— I can already see you smiling at my attempts at consolation, and thinking: such things are of little concern to Dollie; she knows what she wants and has demonstrated this frequently…

I have done a lot of studying here and have completed my deliberations on the fundamental laws of thermoelectricity. I have also come up with a very simple method of determining whether the latent heat of metals can be reduced to the motion of ponderable matter or of electricity, i.e., whether an electrically charged body has a different specific heat from an uncharged one. All of these questions are related to the analysis of the thermoelement. The procedures can be carried out very simply and require no equipment that is not readily available to us.

That's enough for today; any more and my parents will tease me for writing so much without first getting a reply. Best wishes, and looking forward to a happy reunion, your

Albert

From *Albert Einstein–Mileva Marić: The Love Letters,* translated by Shawn Smith, 1992

Einstein and Freud

In 1931 or 1932 Einstein wrote to Sigmund Freud (1856–1939), inviting him to join in forming a "high-level intellectual community" whose moral influence could be brought to bear upon political leaders. "I had rather put these proposals to you than to anyone else in the world," Einstein wrote, "because you are least of all men the dupe of your desires." The two exchanged several letters, written for publication.

Detail of a letter from Freud to Einstein, 1932.

Dear Professor Freud,

I feel elated that through a request of the League of Nations I have been given the unique opportunity to discuss with you those questions which in the present state of world affairs appear to me to be the most important ones facing civilization. Is there a way to liberate mankind from the doom of war? Although it has become common knowledge that because of technological progress a threat to our very existence is the fundamental part of this question, the most ardent efforts at solving it have failed to a frightening degree. Isn't it gratifying that some of those who are practically and professionally concerned with this problem now wish, out of a certain feeling of powerlessness, to learn from the men whose scientific work has given them the objectivity that this subject requires?…

How is it possible that the mass of the people permits itself to become aroused to the point of insanity and eventual self-sacrifice by these means? The answer can only be: man has in him the need to hate and to destroy. This tendency is usually latent, showing itself only in abnormal times, yet it can be awakened relatively easily in periods of stress and inflamed into a mass psychosis. It seems that here lies the deepest problem of the whole mystery, upon which only the great expert in human instincts can shed light.

This leads me to a last question: is it possible to so guide the psychological development of man that it becomes resistant to the psychoses of hate and destruction? I am not thinking only of the so-called uneducated. In my experience, it is much more the so-called intelligentsia who succumb most readily to mass suggestion…

Dear Professor Einstein,

When I learned that you intended to ask me for an exchange of ideas about a topic which greatly interests you and which also is worthy of the interest of others, I gladly consented…You surprised me by proposing the question: what can be done to protect human beings from the fate of war? At first I was scared by the thought of my, I almost said our, incompetence, for this seemed to me to be appropriately a task for statesmen. But then I understood that you did not raise the question as a natural scientist and physicist but as a friend of mankind…

You express your astonishment that it is so easy to create enthusiasm for war in human beings and you suspect that there is something in them, a drive to hate and to destroy, which works in accord with incitement…We suppose that human instincts are of two kinds: either those which seek to preserve and unite—we call them erotic in the sense of Eros in Plato's *Symposium,* or sexual, with conscious overextension of the popular concept of sexuality—and others which seek to destroy and kill; we summarize these as aggressive or destructive instincts. You recognize that this is basically only the theoretical transfiguration of the universally known contrast of love and hate, which perhaps has an essential relationship to the polarity of attraction and repulsion that plays a part in your field. Let us not use too quickly the value judgement of good and bad. Either of these drives is just as indispensable as the other…

If men are commanded to go to war, a number of motives may be present: noble and vulgar ones, those which one loudly declares and others about which one keeps silent…

I hesitate to take advantage of your interest which is concerned with the prevention of war, not with our theories. Yet I would like for a moment to stay with our destructive instinct, a theory whose popularity in no way matches its importance. After some speculation we arrived at the concept that this instinct works within each living being, eventually trying to destroy it and thus to reduce life to the condition of lifeless matter. It indeed deserves the name of death instinct, while the erotic drives represent the effort toward life. The death instinct becomes the destructive instinct when, with the help of special organs, it turns outward, against objects. The living organism so to speak spares its own life by destroying the alien one. But one part of the death instinct remains busy inside the living organism, and we have tried to deduce a great number of normal and pathological phenomena from this internalization of the destructive instinct…

From all of this we conclude for our immediate purposes that there is no prospect of getting rid of the aggressive instinct…

Why are we, you and I and so many others, so indignant about war? Why don't we accept it as we do so many other painful calamities of life? It seems to be a natural occurrence, biologically well founded, and evidently scarcely avoidable. Don't be horrified by my question. For the purpose of exploration one is perhaps permitted to put on a mask of detachment which one does not feel in reality. The answer will be: because every individual has a right to his own life, because war destroys hopeful lives, puts the individual into situations which degrade him, forces him to murder others, and destroys precious things created by human hands…

All this is true and seems so indisputable that one only marvels that war has not yet been condemned by general human consent. Some of the points I have made might be discussed. It might be debated that the community also has a right to the life of its individual members; one cannot condemn all kinds of war equally, and as long as there are empires and nations which are ready for ruthless destruction of others, these others must be armed for war. But let us skip over all this quickly, since it does not answer what you have asked, and I am concerned with something else. I believe that the main reason for our revolt against war is that we cannot do otherwise. We are pacifists because we have to be for organic reasons…My statement requires explanation. I mean this: for all of his history, man has gone through a process of cultural development (I know that some prefer to call it "civilization"). We owe to this process the best we have become and a good part of what we suffer…

Of the psychological characteristics of culture, two seem to be most important: strengthening of the intellect which is beginning to dominate the instincts, and internalization of the aggressive instinct, with all the advantageous and dangerous consequences. Since war in the most glaring way conflicts with the psychological attitudes which result from the cultural process, we must rebel against it; we simply cannot take it anymore. This is not only an intellectual and emotional aversion; it has become to us pacifists a constitutional aversion…

How long do we have to wait for others to become pacifists? This I cannot predict, but perhaps it would not be utopian to hope that the influence of these two circumstances, the cultural attitude and the well-justified fear of the consequences of a future war, will put an end within the foreseeable future to the waging of wars…

From *Why War? The Correspondence between Albert Einstein and Sigmund Freud,* 1932, translated by Fritz and Anna Moellenhoff

Dear Professor Freud,

It is admirable the way the longing to perceive the truth has overcome every other desire in you. You have shown with irresistible clearness how inseparably the combative and destructive instincts are bound up with the amative and vital ones in the human psyche. At the same time a deep yearning for that great consummation, the internal and external liberation of mankind from war, shines out from the

Einstein and the astronomer Charles Edward St. John at Mount Wilson Solar Observatory, California, c. 1931. St. John researched the red shift.

ruthless logic of your expositions. This has been the declared aim of all those who have been honoured as moral and spiritual leaders beyond the limits of their own time and country without exception, from Jesus Christ to Goethe and Kant. Is it not significant that such men have been universally accepted as leaders, in spite of the fact that their efforts to mould the course of human affairs were attended with but small success?

I am convinced that the great men—those whose achievements, even though in a restricted sphere, set them above their fellows—are animated to an over-whelming extent by the same ideals. But they have little influence on the course of political events. It almost looks as if this domain, on which the fate of nations depends, had inevitably to be given over to violence and irresponsibility…

Don't you think that a change might be brought about in this respect by a free association of people whose work and achievements up to date constitute a guarantee of their ability and purity of aim? This international association, whose members would need to keep in touch with each other by a constant interchange of opinions, might, by defining its attitude in the Press—responsibility always resting with the signatories on any given occasion—acquire a considerable and salutary moral influence over the settlement of political questions. Such an association would, of course, be a prey to all the ills which so often lead to degeneration in learned societies, dangers which are inseparably bound up with the imper-fection of human nature. But should not an effort in this direction be risked in spite of this? I look upon the attempt as nothing less than an imperative duty…

from Albert Einstein,
The World as I See It, 1934,
translated by Alan Harris

Sigmund Freud in 1931.

Einstein and the Jews

Both atheists and devout Jews claim that Einstein belongs to them. His attitude toward religion was a complicated mixture of identity with a people and skepticism. The following is excerpted from an address he gave in 1931 on Palestine, later to become Israel.

We—that is to say, the Arabs and ourselves—have got to agree on the main outlines of an advantageous partnership which shall satisfy the needs of both nations. A just solution of this problem and one worthy of both nations is an end no less important and no less worthy of our efforts than the promotion of the work of construction itself…

We are assembled today for the purpose of calling to mind our age-old community, its destiny, and its problems. It is a community of moral tradition, which has always shown its strength and vitality in times of stress. In all ages it has produced men who embodied the conscience of the Western world, defenders of human dignity and justice.

So long as we ourselves care about this community it will continue to exist to the

A 1926 meeting of the International Commission for Intellectual Cooperation of the League of Nations. Einstein is third from left.

benefit of mankind, in spite of the fact that it possesses no self-contained organization. A decade or two ago a group of far-sighted men, among whom Herzl of immortal memory stood out above the rest, came to the conclusion that we needed a spiritual centre in order to preserve our sense of solidarity in difficult times. Thus arose the idea of Zionism and the work of settlement in Palestine, the successful realization of which we have been permitted to witness, at least in its highly promising beginnings.

I have had the privilege of seeing, to my great joy and satisfaction, how much this achievement has contributed to the recovery of the Jewish people, which is exposed, as a minority among the nations, not merely to external dangers, but also to internal ones of a psychological nature...

We need to pay great attention to our relations with the Arabs. By cultivating these carefully we shall be able in future to prevent things from becoming so dangerously strained that people can take advantage of them to provoke acts of hostility. This goal is perfectly within our reach, because our work of construction has been, and must continue to be, carried out in such a manner as to serve the real interests of the Arab population also...

We shall thereby be following not merely the dictates of Providence but also our traditions, which alone give the Jewish community meaning and stability. For that community is not, and must never become, a political one; this is the only permanent source whence it can draw new strength and the only ground on which its existence can be justified.

For the last two thousand years the common property of the Jewish people has consisted entirely of its past. Scattered over the wide world, our nation possessed nothing in common except its carefully guarded tradition. Individual Jews no doubt produced great work, but it seemed as if the Jewish people as a whole had not the strength left for great collective achievements.

Now all that is changed. History has set us a great and noble task in the shape of active cooperation in the building up of Palestine. Eminent members of our race are already at work with all their might on the realization of this aim. The opportunity is presented to us of setting up centres of civilization which the whole Jewish people can regard as its work. We nurse the hope of erecting in Palestine a home of our own national culture which shall help to awaken the near East to new economic and spiritual life.

The object which the leaders of Zionism have in view is not a political but a social and cultural one. The community in Palestine must approach the social ideal of our forefathers as it is laid down in the Bible, and at the same time become a seat of modern intellectual life, a spiritual centre for the Jews of the whole world. In accordance with this notion, the establishment of a Jewish university in Jerusalem constitutes one of the most important aims of the Zionist organization...

For us Jews Palestine is not just a charitable or colonial enterprise, but a problem of central importance for the Jewish people. Palestine is not primarily a place of refuge for the Jews of Eastern Europe, but the embodiment of the re-awakening corporate spirit of the whole Jewish nation. Is it the right moment for this corporate sense to be awakened and strengthened? This is a question to which I feel compelled, not merely by my spontaneous feelings but on rational grounds, to return an unqualified "yes."

Let us just cast our eyes over the history of the Jews in Germany during the past hundred years. A century ago our forefathers, with few exceptions, lived in the ghetto. They were poor, without political rights, separated from the Gentiles by a barrier of religious traditions, habits of life, and legal restrictions; their intellectual development was restricted to their own literature, and they had remained almost unaffected by the mighty advance of the European intellect which dates from the Renaissance. And yet these obscure, humble people had one great advantage over us: each of them belonged in every fibre of his being to a community in which he was completely absorbed, in which he felt himself a fully-privileged member, and which demanded nothing of him that was contrary to his natural habits of thought. Our forefathers in those days were pretty poor specimens intellectually and physically, but socially speaking they enjoyed an enviable spiritual equilibrium.

Then came emancipation, which suddenly opened up undreamed-of possibilities to the individual. Some few rapidly made a position for themselves in the higher walks of business and social life. They greedily lapped up the splendid triumphs which the art and science of the Western world had achieved. They joined in the process with burning enthusiasm, themselves making contributions of lasting value. At the same time they imitated the external forms of Gentile life, departed more and more from their religious and social traditions, and adopted Gentile customs, manners, and habits of thought. It seemed as though they were completely losing their identity in the superior numbers and more highly organized culture of the nations among whom they lived, so that in a few generations there would be no trace of them left. A complete disappearance of Jewish nationality in Central and Western Europe seemed inevitable.

But events turned out otherwise. Nationalities of different race seem to have an instinct which prevents them from fusing. However much the Jews adapted themselves, in language, manners, and to a great extent even in the forms of religion, to the European peoples among whom they lived, the feeling of strangeness between the Jews and their hosts never disappeared. This spontaneous feeling is the ultimate cause of anti-Semitism, which is therefore not to be got rid of by well-meaning propaganda. Nationalities want to pursue their own path, not to blend. A satisfactory state of affairs can be brought about only by mutual toleration and respect.

The first step in that direction is that we Jews should once more become conscious of our existence as a nationality and regain the self-respect that is necessary to a healthy existence. We must learn once more to glory in our ancestors and our history and once again take upon ourselves, as a nation, cultural tasks of a sort calculated to strengthen our sense of the community. It is not enough for us to play a part as individuals in the cultural development of the human race, we must also tackle tasks which only nations as a whole can perform. Only so can the Jews regain social health…

Albert Einstein,
The World as I See It, 1934,
translated by Alan Harris

This section of a 1937–38 mural by Ben Shahn depicts Jewish immigrants, including Einstein, arriving in America.

The moral dilemma of science

The German playwright Bertolt Brecht (1898–1956), like Einstein, was driven from Germany in 1933 and found refuge in the United States. Though both were political leftists, Brecht was critical of Einstein. In 1938 he wrote the play Galileo, *which dramatizes the torment of a scientist whose research threatens the established order, and who is forced by the Inquisition to recant. A 1947 version of the play, written after the bombing of Hiroshima, is more explicitly critical of Einstein.*

Brecht mentioned Einstein in a lecture delivered at the beginning of World War II:

Before the war I heard a truly historic event on the radio: members of the physicist Niels Bohr's institute in Copenhagen were interviewed about a major breakthrough in the field of atomic fission. These researchers reported the discovery of an immense new source of energy. When the interviewer asked whether practical applications of these experiments were possible, he was told, "No, not yet." The interviewer responded with obvious relief: "Thank God! I am convinced that humanity is just not ready to take on such an energy source!" He was obviously thinking of the war industry.

The physicist Albert Einstein does not go that far, although he goes far enough; he wrote the following as a report to future generations about our time. It is to be buried in a time capsule at the [1939] New York World's Fair:

"Our age is rich in inventive minds whose discoveries could make our lives far easier. We use mechanical forces to cross oceans and we also use machine power to spare people all taxing muscular effort. We have learned to fly and we can send reports and news across the world on waves of electricity. And yet the production and distribution of goods is still totally unorganized, so that everyone has to live in fear of being cut out of the economic network. Moreover, people in different countries kill one another at irregular intervals; thus, anyone who considers our future must live in fear. The reason for this is that character and intelligence among the masses are immeasurably inferior to the character and intelligence of the few who make valuable contributions for the community."

If our great advances in conquering nature have contributed so little to human happiness, the reason, according to Einstein, is that human beings in general lack an understanding of how to make use of discoveries and inventions.* They have too little understanding of their own nature. Humanity's ignorance about itself explains why our knowledge of nature is of so little help to us. The monstrous oppression and exploitation of people by people, the slaughters of war, and the indignities of all kinds inflicted in peacetime all over the planet have by now assumed an almost natural quality; mankind proves far less inventive and industrious in dealing with these natural phenomena than with some other kinds. Great wars, for instance, seem as frequent as earthquakes—that is, as natural forces—but while we can deal with earthquakes, we are unable to deal with ourselves. It is obvious that a great deal could be gained if the theater, for instance, or art in general could give us a workable view of the world.

An art that could do this would be capable of affecting human development profoundly; it would no longer merely furnish more-or-less vague impulses, but instead would deliver up the world, the human world, to feeling

and thinking human beings as their field of action.

Bertolt Brecht, 1939,
in Werner Hecht et al., eds.,
Bertolt Brecht Werken (*Works*), vol. 22,
1993, pp. 549–50

In his diaries Brecht recorded a range of mixed feelings about Einstein, modern science, and the bomb. In the 1950s he considered writing a play about Einstein as a companion to Galileo, *but only made a few notes for it.*

March 17, 1942
Reichenbach's lecture at the University of California on *determinism*. Our system of causes is limited by a kind of reproducibility which Einstein once expressed as follows: he described very irregular and rhythmically unstable movements with his finger and said, for instance if the stars moved like that, there would be no astronomy. (Although they would no doubt have good causes for doing so.) Philosophers get irritated by Heisenberg's proposition, according to which points in space and points in time cannot be coordinated. Even if this had identified a limit beyond which descriptive methods theoretically cannot be "improved," the philosophers would still be left with the question of the possibility of description, so that their proposition that nothing happens without cause would still stand. The physicists have overturned it by demonstrating its emptiness; they just abandon it. Grounds that cannot be established theoretically are not grounds for them at all.

Philosophers' inability to imagine *nothingness* naturally no longer prevents physicists from treating *nothing* as *nothing*. All the same, their habit of greeting 0 as an "order of magnitude"

_____
*There is no need here to go into a thorough critique of the technocratic viewpoint of this major scientist. Of course socially useful things are produced by the masses, and the few inventive minds can have no impact on the economic circulation of goods. It is sufficient here to note that Einstein, directly and indirectly, points out our ignorance in social matters.

means that they have a great deal on their conscience. In a system of magnitude 0 may perhaps be adduced as a magnitude—or rather, it can hardly be designated otherwise. But without some "feeling" for dialectics it is impossible to make the logical jump from the other orders of magnitude into that of *non-magnitude*. So space as a quality of matter is something philosophers cannot conceive of. They find it uncanny that space should only be that which is occupied by matter.

Unfortunately, R[eichenbach] does not say a word about all this.

March 18, 1942
I like the world of the physicists. Men change it, and then it looks astonishing. We can appear as the gamblers we are, with our approximations, our to-the-best-of-our-abilities, our dependence on others, on the unknown, on things complete in themselves. So once again a variety of things can lead to success, more than just one path is open. Oddly enough I feel more free in this world than in the old one.

April 13, 1948
…As for the efforts to isolate national socialism intellectually as a series of excesses, exaggerations, what was it that was done to excess, exaggerated? SS leader Heydrich (or was it Kaltenbrunner?) was an "outstanding lover of Bach," Einstein plays in a quartet and is a humanist, and somewhere there are bomb factories working day and night. We read wild west stories; our grandchildren should read wild east stories; pioneers battling with certain tribes.

July 8, 1954
Steff sends me, through very indirect channels, Oppenheimer's long and

Bertolt Brecht in 1931.

thorough piece written in his own defence. This unfortunate man helped to make the first atom bomb when American physicists in World War 2 heard that Hitler had people working on an atom bomb. He and his colleagues were then appalled to find that it had been dropped on Japan. He had moral objections to the hydrogen bomb and now he has been packed off to the wilderness. His document reads as if it was by a man who stands accused by a tribe of cannibals of having refused to go for the meat, and then claims by way of excuse that during the manhunt he was only collecting firewood for the cauldron. What darkness.

May 1955, Warsaw

…[I] questioned [the physicist Leopold] Infeld about Einstein. He stresses how withdrawn he is. "We have to talk more quietly today, my wife is dying in the next room." Infeld: "Einstein is no subject for a play, he has no partner, who are you going to make him talk to?"

I am however interested in a questionnaire relating to conditions in Poland which Einstein is supposed to have sent to Poland via the physicist Nathan.

from Bertolt Brecht,
Journals, 1942–55,
translated by Hugh Rorrison

In his *Galileo*, Bertolt Brecht, who called himself the "Einstein of the new theatrical form," also raises the question of scientists' responsibility for their ideas. Although the play explores the Renaissance struggle between the Church and Galileo, the issues deliberately pertain to modern scientists and the decisions that must be made about the use of their inventions and discoveries.

Actually, the play has three versions. The original, written in 1938, showed a heroic Galileo fighting for the progress against the Inquisition. A second version was written in 1944–45 with Charles Laughton, who helped turn the stage Galileo into a coward and self-centered opportunist. In the preface to this American edition, Brecht wrote: "The atomic age made its debut in Hiroshima while we were in the midst of our work. Overnight the biography of the founder of modern physics read differently. The infernal effect of the great bomb placed the conflict of Galileo with the authorities of his age in a new and sharper light." The numerous changes in this second version, particularly in the recantation

Einstein holding an Einstein puppet.

scene, connect Galileo with contemporary physicists whom Brecht held largely responsible for the nuclear nightmare. A third version of the play makes Galileo an ambiguous composite of the first two, a more complex and interesting figure, even though the first version was closer to historical fact…

Alan J. Friedman and
Carol C. Donley
Einstein as Myth and Muse, 1985

Mythologies

*Einstein sticking out his tongue;
Einstein with windblown hair,
like an elderly madman;
Einstein with a shrewd twinkle
in his eye, laughing at himself
and the world. No man more
completely embodies the modern
image of the eccentric,
irreverent genius.*

Einstein clowns for the camera in one of the most famous photographs of him, 1951.

Myth merges with history

The significant connection between Einstein and the bomb had little to do with $E = Mc^2$ or even physics, but everything to do with the mythic stature of Einstein's image in 1939.

Young refugee physicists in the U.S. such as [Leo] Szilard were vitally concerned that the development of atomic weapons was taking place in Hitler's Germany as well as in the allied nations. A key resource in atomic research was the element uranium, which was uniquely suitable for the work. Szilard, and another physicist, Eugene Wigner… visited Einstein in July 1939…It occurred to the younger physicists that Einstein's name might be the entree to the Washington power structure… A letter to Roosevelt was prepared. That famous letter, signed by Einstein and dated August 2, warned that "the element uranium may be turned into a new and important source of energy…" That letter is a serious basis for connecting Einstein with the development of the atomic bomb.

Einstein was involved not because he had made contributions to the development of atomic energy or had supported that work…but because his fame would facilitate reaching world leaders…

The physicists knew that Einstein was useful because of his image, conjuring up the full powers of science in an age when the applicability of theoretical physics to practical warfare was still questionable. Alexander Sachs describes Einstein's contribution with terms appropriate to a mythological being: "We really only needed Einstein in order to provide Szilard with a halo, as Szilard was almost unknown in the United States."

Today's popular myth has taken that literal link, as well as the much less plausible connection between relativity and the bomb, as the central example in a vision of the relations between science and society. After the bomb was dropped on Japan in 1945, science itself took on a new and darker significance in the world. Albert Einstein, who had provided the image of the ultimate scientist with his theory of relativity, now became a key image of the new danger posed by science. Einstein's links to the bombs, both the vastly overstressed association of $E = Mc^2$ and the authentic one of the letter of 1939, were a convenient focus for discussions of the moral responsibility or irresponsibility of science.

The shift in attitude toward Einstein, and science in general, can be seen in both serious and popular literature… Rebecca West [wrote of Einstein]…in 1931:

One perceived that the hierarchies of the earth, in spite of his high place among them, were invisible to him. He held the stuff of life towards the light in some way so that that kind of embroidery did not show…

The myth in fiction and non-fiction

In the decade preceding World War II, Einstein was the personification of science, and atomic physics was a poorly understood but central topic of science. $E = Mc^2$ was a short equation and even if it was not the totality of his great theory of relativity, the public took it to be so. Since 1919, when Einstein had become famous, scientists and science fiction writers discussing atomic energy had used $E = Mc^2$ to illustrate how much energy was involved with radioactivity…

The mythical direct connection between Einstein, relativity, and the threat of nuclear holocaust was thus easily made immediately after World War II. The *Time* [magazine] cover story of July 1, 1946, contains all the elements, both factual and fictitious, of that connection. The essay begins with photographs and a description of the planned Bikini Island atomic bomb tests. Then: *"The Genius.* Through the incomparable blast and flame that will follow, there will be dimly discernible, to those who are interested in cause & effect in history, the features of a shy, almost saintly childlike little man with the soft brown eyes, the drooping facial lines of a world-weary hound, and hair like an aurora borealis." The biographic sketch of Einstein and his supposed connections to the bomb present the full legend…

The modern myth about science and society…has two facets which are clearly present in the *Time* essay on Einstein and the bomb. The first facet is the potential of science to liberate great power, represented by Einstein's $E = Mc^2$, making the bomb possible… Fundamental science did lead to the release of that energy and then to building of the bomb, so the myth has a general validity despite the inaccuracy of the central example. The juxtaposition of the three images—Einstein, the equation, and the bomb—is now a widely recognized icon, repeated over and over again in post World War II literature, both fiction and prose…

The second aspect of the general myth is that powers are released by science so suddenly that society has no chance to consider the potential dangers. Einstein's image is of an old, tired man, full of great sorrow for the harm he has inadvertently released. As we have seen, in the period of fifty years between the first research on radioactivity (and coincidentally $E = Mc^2$) and the realization of the bomb, the potential dangers and benefits of atomic energy were widely discussed, not only by scientists, but by popularizers and fiction authors [who]… had considered the general classes of side effects: economic, political, military, and social. In the early 1940's, the discussions in science fiction ran ahead of the developments in science in technical details as well…Immediately after the war, science fiction stories abounded about the aftermath of a world-wide nuclear holocaust…The attention paid by science fiction to the potentials of atomic energy, from 1908 until the actual utilization of atomic energy in 1945, is a convincing demonstration that the implications of *this* power released by science could have been thoroughly and publicly considered. The aspect of the general myth about science and society, that change occurs too rapidly for careful study, is contradicted by the decades of serious and popular examination of atomic energy…

Einstein as a personification of intellect

In addition to its presumed role in atomic energy, the public image of Albert Einstein has come to represent intelligence in general, and the scientific mind in particular. That image is consistent with a national stereotype of scientists as distinctly odd people…

Portraits of Einstein from mass circulation material in the 1970's present certain prominent recurring features. Einstein appears throughout as a very old man; the symbols $E = Mc^2$ are used to represent his major work and nuclear power; and Einstein is used to represent

supreme intellect, which is out of reach of the ordinary mind. The misleading or inaccurate nature of these features has not diminished their importance in making a powerful cultural myth out of Einstein's image…

Einstein's aged face has come to represent the ambiguity of our attitude toward intellect: respected yet feared, a force that is mysterious and perhaps not under control…The real Einstein at the time he was completing the Special Theory of Relativity [is] not a frail old man at all, but a rather handsome young fellow, twenty-six years old…The Einstein who "discovers" relativity in popular image is at least forty years older than the Einstein who invented relativity in fact. The association of wisdom with age is a longstanding notion, however, and so if Einstein is to represent intellectual wisdom for our culture, he had better be much older than a tender twenty-six years…

Status of the mythic image

We have examined the image of Albert Einstein as a cultural icon, and seen the range of uses of that image, from the humorous to the tragic. Einstein's image has not by itself created the vision of science in 20th-century culture, but it has been adopted by that culture to represent the intellectual enterprise.

In some way, however, the real Einstein has at least modified the image of science. In pre-20th-century debates on the moral responsibility of science, symbolized by Mary Shelley's Frankenstein, the dangers to society from the scientist were in large part due to the classic sins of man: pride, greed, selfishness. But the conception of Einstein is closer to that of a saint—he is seen to radiate cosmic humility, generosity,

Einstein at work.

of the man, but of the society, or of society's abuse of knowledge.

By limiting its image of science largely to one individual, our culture has also reinforced some of its specific prejudices about intellect. First, no other age, sex, or skin color seems to fit so well with genius, so that a young, black woman must overcome an image as well as more concrete barriers, if she is to be encouraged and recognized as a scientist. Discrimination in education and in science is certainly not supported by Einstein's biography, but the use of Einstein as a sole image makes it easier for society to educate youth to maintain old predilections. The same sole-image prejudice attaches Einstein's foibles and failures (particularly in politics) to science and genius as a whole.

Second, since Einstein's field of science was mathematical physics, that realm of endeavor is *the* prestige field in which to look for great intellectual achievement. The arts, poetry, politics, and even other sciences are perceived with less status, in part due to Einstein's eminence. We look to physical science for solutions to societies' problems with more seriousness, and more money, than we might if our culture had happened to choose a philosopher, a poet, or a psychologist for its symbol of intellect.

And finally, since Einstein is not supposed to be understandable to normal intellects, Einstein's image supports the anti-intellectual notion that higher thought is not fit for general public consumption…

This survey of the cultural image of Albert Einstein raises questions of society's response to ideas, and to dramatically gifted individuals. Certainly Einstein's person and image have been used to express and support concepts

unselfishness. The *Time* magazine Einstein centennial cover from 1979 illustrates this aspect of Einstein's image. Gone are the mushroom cloud and warships of the 1946 cover. An Einstein of the same approximate age as shown in 1946 now has galaxies and nebulae for an environment. Thus the evil coming from science, exemplified by the transformation of gentle Einstein's $E = Mc^2$ into the terror of atomic holocaust, can be seen as a failing not

such as "everything is relative," which in reality he would never have accepted. The myth of science unleashing powers without warning has hindered rational consideration of the role of science in society. Society's guilt over such processes as the evolution of nuclear weapons is inappropriately assuaged if a single, saintly member of society can somehow be imagined to bear a large share of the responsibility. These facets of Einstein's existence have been far more powerful in the culture at large than have his ideas and his actual biography. The uses and celebrations of those realities in works by many artists and authors... demonstrate that fruitful inspiration can come from fact as well as from myth.

Alan J. Friedman and
Carol C. Donley,
Einstein as Myth and Muse, 1985

Einstein and art

Soon,...artists introduced styles that resonated with the distant sounds of a fast-approaching new physical theory about the world...In the late 1920s Lyonel Feininger created images consonant with Einstein's blurred interrelationship between space and mass by continuing the planes of his solid objects into the space around them...

The scientific community was struck speechless when first confronted in 1915 by Einstein's integrated energy-mass and warped spacetime equations. Pressed to create a visual metaphor to help his audience understand his insight, Einstein replied, in effect, that "there is none." In trying to explain the difficulty, even Einstein could not express in language what he had envisioned: "We cannot use in the general relativity theory the mechanical scaffolding of parallel and perpendicular rods and synchronized

clocks...Our world is not Euclidean. The geometrical nature of our world is shaped by masses and their velocities."

As if to emphasize his unusual thought processes and lack of reliance on language, Einstein...wrote, "The words or the language, as they are written or spoken, do not seem to play any role in my mechanism of thought."

Spacetime, quantum jumping, and spacetime warped by mass-energy were so far from ordinary experience that the ordinary human mind, with very few exceptions, could not conceive of them. For the first time since natural philosophers began to inquire into the nature of the universe, scientists had created models of reality that humans, the most visual of animals, could not visualize. The concepts of general relativity, it seemed, could be precisely expressed only by the use of abstract mathematical symbols...

The failure of language to explicate the new paradigm of physics coincided with the introduction of a completely new, nonrepresentational form of art... Abstract art, like the abstract mathematics upon which the new physics depended, could not be translated into an easily understandable visual model. Non-Euclidean geometry, the unimaginable arcane space supposedly confined to mathematics, became the new basis of physical reality, and art without an image became a major new style in art...

During the second decade of the twentieth century Kandinsky, the first abstract painter, assumed that space had an inherent geometry and organized many of his later abstract works geometrically...Mondrian...asserted as a basic principle of his art that "force is geometry," about the same time Einstein's equations declared that space is geometry and the force of gravity is due to the shape of spacetime. A leading avant-garde artist and the most prominent physicist both concluded at the same time that space was in fact a geometry and force was due to this feature of space…

Modern art also anticipated Einstein's discovery that gravitational force is an illusion…Painters began to portray people flying about, freed from the cloying hold of earth's gravitational pull. Marc Chagall, in particular, went beyond painting acrobats and jugglers as his immediate predecessors had done and made floating, flying, and levitation common sights in his art…

Escher also challenged traditional beliefs regarding gravity. In a clever cardboard cutout entitled *Three Spheres I* (1945), he demonstrated, using projective geometrical lines, the effect of gravity crushing and distorting mass. From the traditional perspectivist point of view, three spheres appear to be piled upon one another. The weight of the top two spheres appears to flatten the one below, graphically showing the distorting effects of gravity. When the viewer shifts perspective, however, and considers *Three Spheres I* from another angle, what was perceived to be mass distorted by gravity turns out to be nothing but three-dimensional illusion made from a two-dimensional cardboard cutout. By simply adding another dimen-

sion to the monolinear view imposed by perspective, he takes the viewer behind the facade of three-dimensional gravity…

Alexander Calder, like Rodin before him, broke up the central mass of sculpture and fragmented it into many different pieces. Also, like Rodin, he eliminated the visible center of gravity rooted in mass…In 1932, with his first mobile Calder lifted sculpture right off the floor, defying gravity and deemphasizing weight. Motion and sculpture (energy and mass) had hitherto seemed antithetical; now Calder found a way to express their binary relationship. Further, he suspended the mass of his work in space in a permanent free-fall. By literally hanging mass in space, for the first time ever, Calder disconnected sculpture from its pedestal. By meticulously balancing the density and mass of his mobiles so that they could be affected by something as insubstantial as a breeze, Calder made sculptures like his *Lobster Trap and Fish Tail* (1939) that were more like particles responding in a field of force than like a mass dominating empty space.

During the last forty years, unconsciously and consciously, sculptors seem to have thoroughly integrated Einstein's insights and worldview.

Leonard Shlain,
Art and Physics: Parallel Visions in Space, Time, and Light,
1991

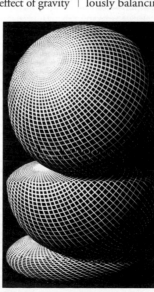

M. C. Escher, *Three Spheres I*, 1945.

Chronology

1879 March 14: birth of Albert Einstein, Ulm, Germany, son of Hermann and Pauline Einstein

1880 The family moves to Munich, Germany

1881 Birth of Maja, Einstein's sister

1885–88 Primary school

1888–94 Attends Luitpold *Gymnasium* (high school), Munich, but leaves without completing diploma

1894 June: the family moves to Milan, then Pavia, Italy

1894 December: joins his parents in Pavia

1895 Fails entrance examination for the Zurich Polytechnic Institute (ETH)

1896 Studies for the Polytechnic in cantonal school, Aarau, Switzerland

1896–1900 Studies at the Polytechnic; meets Mileva Marić

1901 Takes Swiss citizenship; works at odd teaching jobs

1902 Mileva gives birth to a daughter (presumed to have died as a baby); fails her final examinations at the Polytechnic; Einstein hired at the Swiss patent office in Bern; death of Hermann Einstein

1903 Marries Mileva Marić; publishes several papers on the fundamentals of thermodynamics

1904 Birth of Hans Albert Einstein (dies 1973)

1905 Publishes five papers, including one on the quantum theory of light and another that establishes the special theory of relativity, to which he adds a postscript containing the famous equation $E = Mc^2$

1907 Develops the general theory of relativity

1908 Appointed *Privatdozent* (an instructor paid by his students) at Bern University

1909 Appointed professor of theoretical physics at the University of Zurich

1910 Birth of Eduard Einstein (dies 1965)

1911–12 With wife and children moves to Prague, teaches at German University there; meets the physicist Paul Ehrenfest

1912 Returns to Zurich and collaborates with the mathematician Marcel Grossmann on the general theory of relativity

1914 Appointed professor at the University of Berlin; becomes a member of the Prussian Academy of Sciences; signs an antimilitary petition; Mileva returns to Zurich with their two sons; World War I begins

1916 Publishes the general theory of relativity

1917 First studies of cosmology

1918 Einstein supports the liberal Weimar Republic in Germany; World War I ends

1919 Eddington expedition confirms the general theory of relativity; Einstein becomes famous; he divorces Mileva and marries his cousin Elsa

1920 Antisemitic campaign begins against Einstein

1921 Series of travels, especially to the United States, to raise funds for the founding of Hebrew University of Jerusalem

1922 Wins Nobel Prize

1923 Travels to Palestine; resigns from the International Committee on Intellectual Cooperation of the League of Nations

1925 Travels to South America

1927 At Solvay Congress disputes quantum theory with Niels Bohr and others

1930 Visits the United States; in California meets the astronomer Edwin Hubble

1931 Returns to California; invited to join the Institute for Advanced Study, Princeton University, New Jersey

1933 Hitler comes to power; Einstein settles briefly in Belgium; emigrates to the United States with wife and becomes a fellow of the Institute for Advanced Study

1934 Actively assists German Jewish refugees; step-daughter Margot moves to Princeton; death of step-daughter Ilse

1939 Writes to President Franklin D. Roosevelt concerning the possibility of building a nuclear weapon; joined in Princeton by his sister, Maja; World War II begins

1940 Becomes a United States citizen

1945 America explodes atom bombs at Hiroshima and Nagasaki, Japan; end of World War II

1946 Becomes chairman of the Emergency Committee of Atomic Scientists, a pacifist group; supports arms control

1948 Death of Mileva in Zurich

1952 Declines an invitation to serve as president of the State of Israel

1953 Speaks out against anticommunist McCarthyism in the United States, and supports the physicist J. Robert Oppenheimer

1955 April 18: death of Einstein

Further Reading

BY ALBERT EINSTEIN

Albert Einstein: Philosopher-Scientist, ed. P. A. Schilpp (1949), repr. 1988.

Albert Einstein: The Human Side; New Glimpses from His Archives, ed. H. Dukas and B. Hoffmann, 1979.

Autobiographical Notes: A Centennial Edition, ed. P. A. Schilpp, 1991.

The Autobiography of Albert Einstein, trans. M. Green, 1992.

The Born–Einstein Letters: Correspondence between Albert Einstein and Max and Hedwig Born from 1916 to 1955, 1971.

The Collected Papers of Albert Einstein, ed. J. Stachel et al., trans. A. Beck et al., 8 vols. of a projected 25, 1987–.

Einstein, the Man, the Jew: Excerpts from His Articles, Speeches, and Statements, 1955.

Essays in Physics, 1950.

Essays in Science, 1934.

The Evolution of Physics: The Growth of Ideas from Early Concepts to Relativity and Quanta, with L. Infeld, 1961.

The Expanded Quotable Einstein, ed. A. Calaprice, 2000.

Ideas and Opinions, ed. C. Seelig, 1954.

The Joys of Research, ed. W. Shropshire, Jr., 1981.

Living Philosophies, with J. Dewey, J. Jeans, et al., 1931.

The Meaning of Relativity: Four Lectures Delivered at Princeton University, 1923.

Origins of the General Theory of Relativity, 1933.

Out of My Later Years, 1950.

The Quotable Einstein, ed. A. Calaprice, 1996.

Relativity, 1947.

Why War? The Correspondence between Albert Einstein and Sigmund Freud, 1978.

The World as I See It, 1934.

ON ALBERT EINSTEIN

Bernstein, H., *Celebrities of Our Time; Interviews,* 1924.

Bernstein, J., *Einstein,* 1973.

Breithaupt, J., *Einstein: A Beginner's Guide,* 2000.

Brian, D., *Einstein: A Life,* 1996.

Cahn, W., *Einstein: A Pictorial Biography,* 1955.

Cassidy, D. C., *Einstein and Our World,* 1995.

Clark, R. W., *Einstein: The Life and Times, An Illustrated Biography,* 1984.

Fine, A., *The Shaky Game: Einstein, Realism, and the Quantum Theory,* 2d ed., 1996.

Fisher, D. E., *The Ideas of Einstein,* 1980.

Fölsing, A., *Albert Einstein: A Biography,* trans. E. Osers, 1997.

Frank, P., *Einstein: His Life and Times,* 1953.

French, P., ed., *Einstein: A Centenary Volume,* 1979.

Highfield, R., and Carter, R., *The Private Lives of Albert Einstein,* 1993.

Hoffmann, B., with Dukas, H., *Albert Einstein: Creator and Rebel,* 1972.

Holton, G., and Elkana, Y., eds., *Albert Einstein: Historical and Cultural Perspectives,* 1982.

Infeld, L., *Albert Einstein: His Work and Its Influence on Our World,* 1950.

Kantha, S. S., *An Einstein Dictionary,* 1996.

Lightman, A. P., *Einstein's Dreams,* 1994.

MacLeish, A., *Einstein,* 1929.

Pais, A., *Einstein Lived Here: Essays for the Layman,* 1994.

———, *Subtle Is the Lord...,* 1982.

Paterniti, M., *Driving Mr. Albert: A Trip across America with Einstein's Brain,* 2000.

Paul, I., *Science, Theology, and Einstein,* 1982.

Sayen, J., *Einstein in America: The Scientist's Conscience in the Age of Hitler and Hiroshima,* 1985.

Seelig, C., *Albert Einstein: A Documentary Biography,* trans. M. Savill, 1956.

Sugimoto, K., *Albert Einstein: A Photographic Biography,* trans. B. Harshaw, 1989.

Wheeler, J. A., *Albert Einstein: His Strength and His Struggle,* 1980.

Will, C. M., *Was Einstein Right?,* 1987.

Winteler-Einstein, M., "Albert Einstein—A Biographical Sketch," ms., 1924, excerpts published in *The Collected Papers,* vol. I.

ON PHYSICS

D'Abro, A., *The Rise of the New Physics,* 2 vols., 1951.

Capra, F., *The Tao of Physics,* 1980.

Feynman, R., *The Character of Physical Law,* 1967.

Gribbin, J., *In Search of Schrödinger's Cat: Quantum Physics and Reality,* 1984.

———, *Schrödinger's Kittens and the Search for Reality: Solving the Quantum Mysteries,* 1995.

Heisenberg, W., *Physics and Philosophy,* 1959.

Pagels, H., *The Cosmic Code,* 1982.

Péter, R., *Playing with Infinity,* 1957.

Toulmin, S., and Goodfield, J., *The Architecture of Matter,* 1962.

Zukav, G., *The Dancing Wu Li Masters,* 1980.

List of Illustrations

Index

Photograph Credits

Text Credits

Françoise Balibar is professor of physics at the University of Paris VII
and editor of the French-language edition of the *Selected Works of Einstein*
(6 vols.) Other publications include *La Science d cristal* (*The Science of Cystals*),
and two volumes in the *philosophies* series of the Presses Universitaires de France,
Galilée, Newton lus par Einstein (*Galileo and Newton as Seen by Einstein*) *and
Einstein 1905*. She is co-author with J.-M. Lévy-Lebond of a
textbook on quantum mechanics and with N. Robatel of
La Science en Poésie (*The Sciences in Poetry*).

Translated from the French by David J. Baker and Dorie B. Baker;
see Credits for sources of some quotations

First published in the United Kingdom in 2005 by
Thames & Hudson Ltd, 181A High Holborn,
London WC1V 7QX

www.thamesandhudson.com

British Library Cataloguing-in-Publication Data
A catalogue record for this book is available from the British Library

ISBN-13:   978-0-500-30117-3

ISBN-10:   0-500-30117-4

Printed and bound in Italy by Editoriale Lloyd, Trieste